l Shaddai, God Almighty, I want to tr
n fully, wholeheartedly, with everythin
t You know this can wage war wit
g desire to be certain, to understan
d to control. It feels like there are
ny unknowns in my life, but thank
n that You are constant, the sam
terday, today and forever. You know
e dreams, desires, and hopes for my fut
ten, I want to run ahead of You an
e all these happen. But I don't want t
n on my own understanding; I wa
lean on You. I know the best place
is in Your will. I c
de me, revealing o
ether it's a small step or
e t obey. I know that each step o
I0824139

El Shaddai, God Almighty, I want to
You fully, wholeheartedly, with everythi
But You know this can wage war w
my desire to be certain, to understa
and to control. It feels like there are
many unknowns in my life, but than
You that You are constant, the Sa
yesterday, today, and forever. You kno
have dreams, desires, and hopes for my l
Often, I want to run ahead of You a
make all these happen. But I don't want
lean on my own understanding; I w
to lean on You. I know the best plac
be is in Your will. I can count on You
guide me, revealing one step at a ti
whether it's a small step or a big on
... I know that each step

A GIFT FOR
FROM
DATE

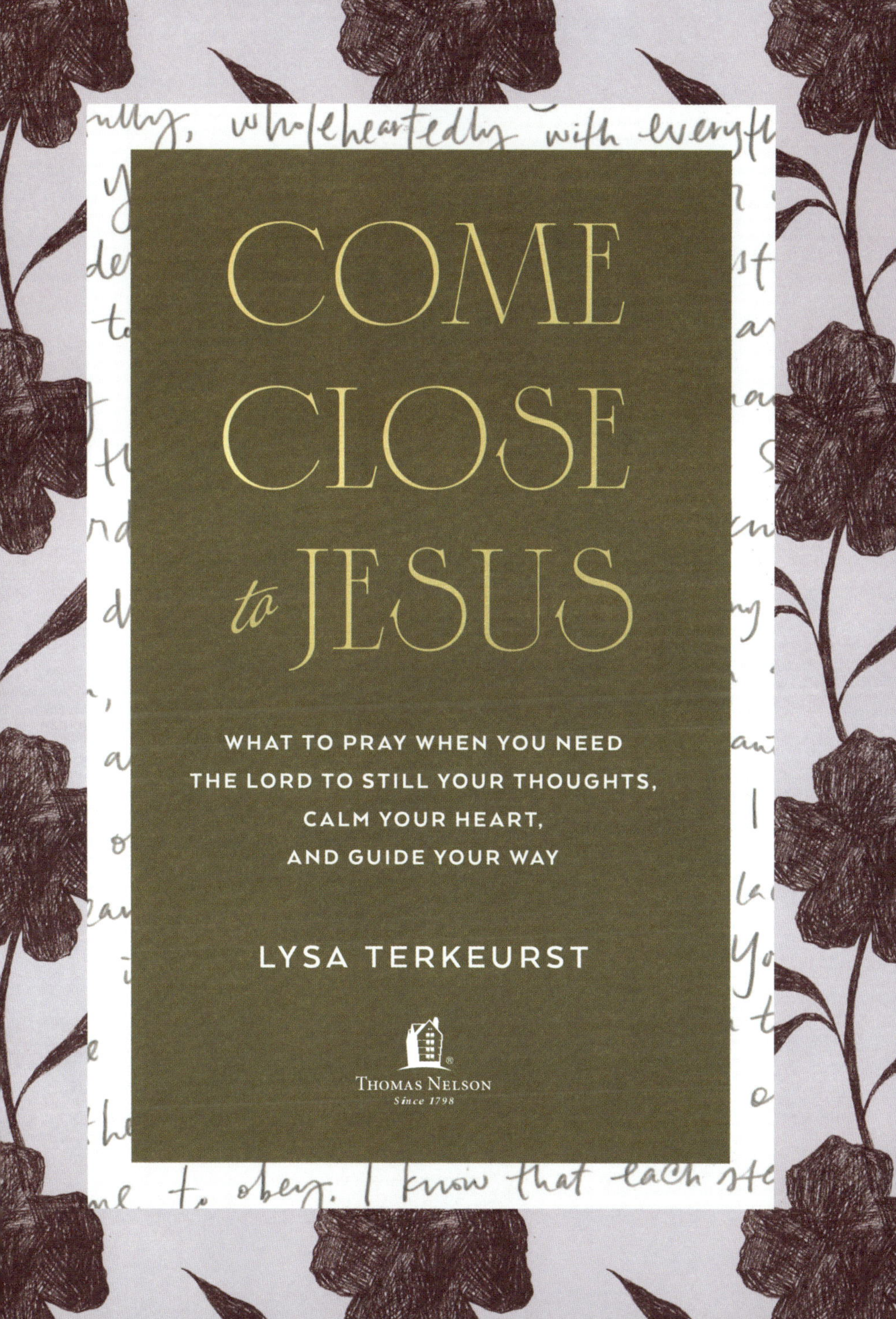
COME CLOSE to JESUS
WHAT TO PRAY WHEN YOU NEED THE LORD TO STILL YOUR THOUGHTS, CALM YOUR HEART, AND GUIDE YOUR WAY
LYSA TERKEURST
THOMAS NELSON
Since 1798

Come Close to Jesus

Published by Thomas Nelson, 501 Nelson Place, Nashville, TN 37214, USA. Thomas Nelson is a registered trademark of HarperCollins Christian Publishing, Inc.

Thomas Nelson titles may be purchased in bulk for educational, business, fundraising, or sales promotional use. For information, please email SpecialMarkets@ThomasNelson.com.

Cover design: Riley Moody
Interior design: Lori Lynch and Riley Moody

ISBN 978-1-4002-5458-3 (HC)
ISBN 978-1-4002-5449-1 (audiobook)
ISBN 978-1-4002-5459-0 (eBook)

HarperCollins Publishers, Macken House, 39/40 Mayor Street Upper, Dublin 1, D01 C9W8, Ireland
(https://www.harpercollins.com)

Printed in India

25 26 27 28 29 REP 10 9 8 7 6 5 4 3 2 1

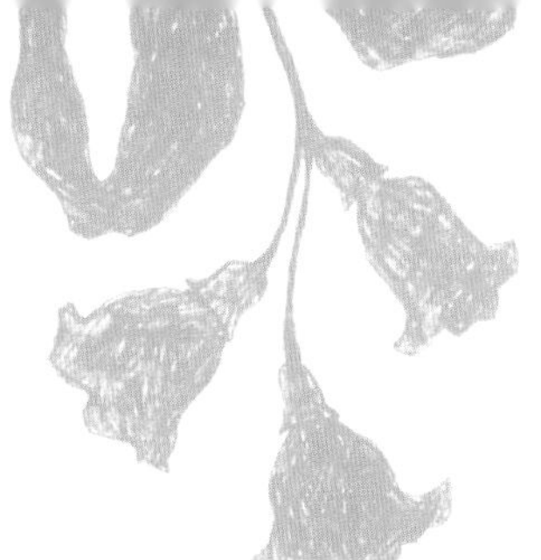

CONTENTS

This book is dedicated to Mel, Candace, and Jenn . . . the women who helped pray me into the life I now love.

INTRODUCTION

I've never felt like I'm terrific at praying. I love God with all my heart, and I desire to keep growing closer to Him. I want to hear from God, and I fully acknowledge how important it is to go to Him with everything I face. But more often than I'd like to admit, when I start to pray, I feel distracted. My brain wants to process what's happening in my life rather than give it to Jesus in prayer. I so often feel like my mind is a swirling mix of confusion about one situation, a desire to prove my point with another issue, gratitude because some things are going well, and, quite honestly, frustration over the fact that some people who cause a lot of hurt just seem to get away with it.

I am confronted regularly with the ways life never seems to settle down; between my own life and the lives of the people I love, it rarely feels like it's all going right at the same time. My heart is full of all kinds of feelings, and my mind is in overdrive trying to figure out so many things—which sometimes spirals me into worry, fear, and confusion.

It doesn't feel awesome for a Bible teacher to admit that. But I'm also a gal just like you, trying to honor God, love my people, and not get overwhelmed with all the circumstances that come at me each day.

Sometimes when I try to sit with my heavenly Father, I want to apologize for all the chaos I bring into my time with Him.

I can easily land in a place of feeling ashamed of these swirling questions and uncertainties and fears. Anyone else? And that's a dangerous place for us to be. Because you know what we sometimes do when we're feeling ashamed, too much of a mess, or frustrated by too many things not going the way we hoped they would? We simply avoid Jesus and try to muddle along on our own.

But that's the exact opposite of what Jesus wants us to do. So can we decide right now that through the reflections and prayers in this book and the prayers from our hearts, we won't do that? We won't run away; we'll run to Jesus.

We'll do what Jesus invites us to do—come close to Him.

All those things you're wondering if you should talk to Jesus about? Yes—to all of them. Here are a few verses to remind you of how precious you are to Him, right here and right now.

He promises nothing can separate you from His love:

For I am convinced that neither death nor life, neither angels nor demons, neither the present nor the future, nor any powers, neither height nor depth, nor anything else in all creation, will be able to separate us from the love of God that is in Christ Jesus our Lord. (Romans 8:38–39)

He promises when you're weak, He's strong:

But he said to me, "My grace is sufficient for you, for my power is made perfect in weakness." Therefore I will boast all the more gladly about my weaknesses, so that Christ's power may rest on me. (2 Corinthians 12:9)

He promises He will carry your burdens:

"Come to me, all you who are weary and burdened, and I will give you rest." (Matthew 11:28)

He promises to be the well of living water when we feel spiritually dry and emotionally drained:

"Let anyone who is thirsty come to me and drink. Whoever believes in me, as Scripture has said, rivers of living water will flow from within them." (John 7:37–38)

He promises to be our Counselor and Comforter:

"But the Comforter (Counselor, Helper, Intercessor, Advocate, Strengthener, Standby), the Holy Spirit, Whom the Father will send in My name [in My place, to represent Me and act on My behalf], He will teach you all things. And He will cause you to recall (will remind you of, bring to your remembrance) everything I have told you." (John 14:26 AMPC)

Coming close to Jesus through prayer is one of His greatest gifts to us. We don't have to carry our burdens and worries alone. We aren't limited to our own resources for strength or wisdom. We don't have to be ashamed of the chaos that might be swirling in our minds or in our lives. I want you to know that He is not disappointed in you because your prayers haven't been more consistent or elaborate. He simply wants you to place more and more of your life into His very capable hands. He loves every second you spend with Him. But most of all He loves you.

God's grace is the sweetest when we acknowledge that we want more in our relationship with Him. He loves His children who come tumbling and stumbling into time with Him. And He wants you to know that prayer is the perfect connection between all you need and the wondrous love He has for you.

In each entry, you'll find a scripture and a nugget of wisdom from what God has been teaching me about stilling my thoughts, calming my mind, and being guided by His wisdom. I have written out prayers for each one of these situations and invite you to pray your own prayers as well.

In the last section of the book, you'll find scriptural prayers for certain situations and people that I've written out just for you. I know you'll love learning how to pray powerful prayers using God's own words.

Sometimes, the hardest part of implementing a fresh rhythm in our lives is getting started. I hope my prayers are just the beginning of you growing and thriving as you experience the Lord every day.

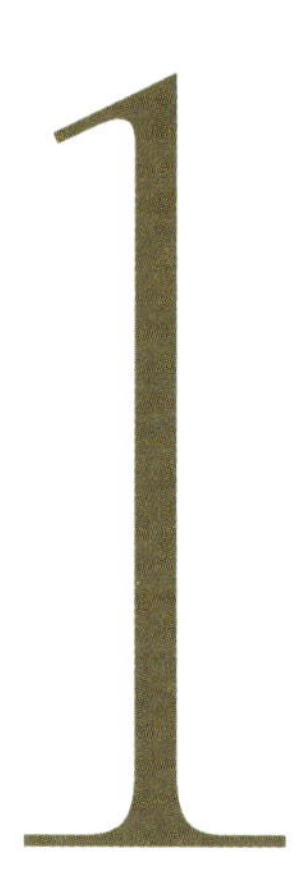

GOD, I WANT TO SEE YOU

"Blessed are the pure in heart,
for they will see God."

MATTHEW 5:8

My heart was crying out to see evidence of God's reality in my life. I wanted to experience His presence and walk in the assurance that He saw me, heard me, and wanted to know me.

When I read Matthew 5:8, the words compelled me to start praying it over my life. This verse doesn't say that only a perfect person will see God. No, the "pure in heart"—the one who really wants to pursue God—*will* see Him. I decided that I would start looking for God with greater intentionality throughout my day. I would tune in to my own life experiences and start living with expectation that I would see Him.

It's now been more than twenty years since I started praying this prayer.

And I'm different because of learning to practice the presence of Jesus and experience Him daily. It has been a purposeful, daily pursuit of Him. I look for Him in unexpected places. I don't see coincidences as chance. And I don't think good things happen because of good luck. It's the Lord. Working. Showing. Guiding. Revealing. Through the good. Through the not so good. And through everything in between.

I invite you to pray this prayer each day as you, too, intentionally choose to come close to Jesus.

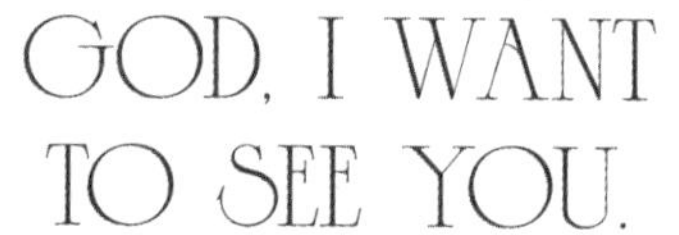

GOD, I WANT TO SEE YOU.

God, I want to hear You.

God, I want to know You.

God, I want to follow hard after You.

And I know . . .

God, You are good.

You are good to me.

You are good at being God.

Therefore, I trade my will for Your will because I'm assured that You will guide me through this.

Thank You that I don't have to figure everything out.

IN JESUS' NAME,

AMEN.

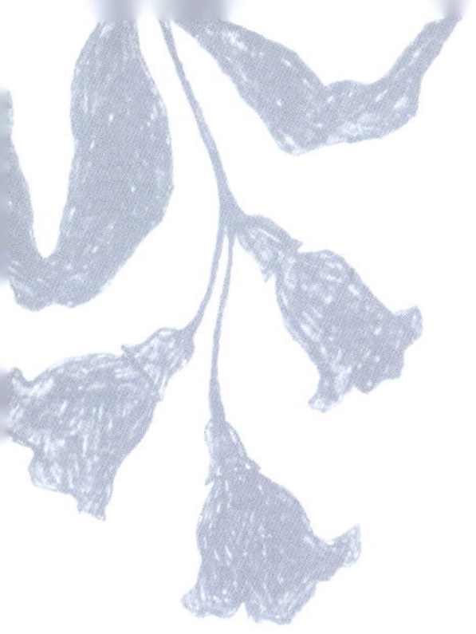

PRAYER IN ACTION

Declare what your mindset and actions will be for the days to come: "I'm intentionally going to look for God every day as I notice the evidence all around me of His goodness and faithfulness."

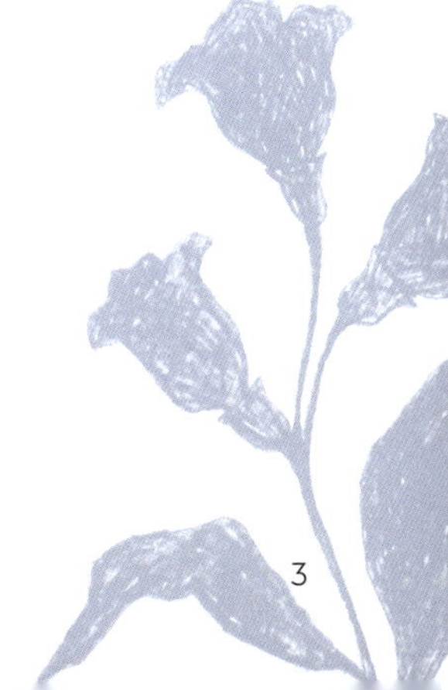

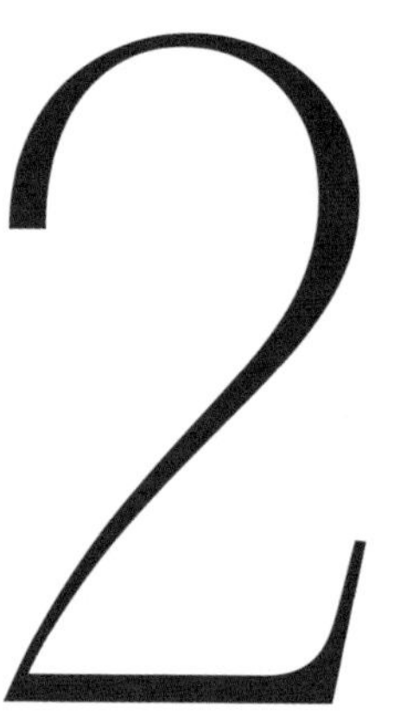

JUST THE NEXT STEP

Trust in the LORD with all your heart and lean not on your own understanding;
in all your ways submit to him, and he will make your paths straight.

PROVERBS 3:5–6

God is teaching me so much about really trusting Him. Fully. Completely. Wholeheartedly.

Though the path I'm on may feel uncertain right now, He's faithful to shed just enough light for me to see the very next step. And this isn't Him being mysterious—this is a great demonstration of His mercy. Instead of bombarding Him with my suggestions or projections, clenching my fists, and reaching for control, I simply need to embrace and obey the very next thing He shows me. And then the next.

Because here's what I know about myself: If God showed me too much revelation through an exact blueprint of where I was headed, I might panic if His plan didn't match what I desperately wanted. Or I might be tempted to take control and make things happen on my own. On the flip side, if He showed me too little, never revealing Himself or His guidance, I'd be paralyzed with the thought that He'd abandoned me.

In His kindness, God gives each of us just enough revelation to keep going today. Most days, this revelation is in the form of an invitation from Him to be fully obedient to Him right now. If I read a Scripture verse, I can feel a prodding in my heart: *Lysa, are you being obedient to Me in this?* Or as I listen to wise counsel, I am challenged: *Lysa, are you willing to implement what is being suggested to you in this situation?* Often my confusion isn't because God is being mysterious; it's because I'm not being obedient.

As I enter this brand-new day, I'm seeking Him rather than trying to figure out His plan. Instead of filling the gaps of the unknown with my suggestions to God, I'm placing my trust in Him.

We don't have to know it all to trust Him completely. We can take it one day at a time. One step at a time. One act of obedience at a time. One sliver of light at a time.

EL SHADDAI, GOD ALMIGHTY,

I want to trust You, fully, wholeheartedly, with everything. But You know that this can wage war with my desire to be certain, to understand, and to control.

It feels like there are too many unknowns in my life, but thank You that You are constant, the same yesterday, today, and forever.

You know I have dreams, desires, and hopes for my future. Often, I want to run ahead of You and make all these happen. But I don't want to lean on my own understanding; I want to lean on You.

I know the best place to be is in Your will. I can count on You to guide me, revealing one step at a time. Whether it's a small step or a big one, help me to obey. I know that each step of obedience increases my faith in You. I want to be someone who lives every day in step with You.

IN JESUS' NAME,
AMEN.

PRAYER IN ACTION

Take a walk and notice your footsteps or footprints. As you walk, repeat, "Lord, I am living in step with You."

CREATE SPACE FOR THE GREAT COMMANDMENT

Jesus replied: "'Love the Lord your God with all your heart and with all your soul and with all your mind.' This is the first and greatest commandment. And the second is like it: 'Love your neighbor as yourself.'"

MATTHEW 22:37–39

One of the most loving things we can do for others is create a space where they know they're safe to reveal their real struggles and hurts. Around a table. On a walk. Maybe even on a road trip. Initiating those moments where togetherness says, "You belong. You have a place. You have a voice. You have people who love you just as you are, right now, in your struggle."

When you're hurting, it can feel isolating when you aren't sure how to talk about the hard things or who can safely hold your honest thoughts. But having God's Spirit in us allows us to love people who are hurting, empathize with their pain, and acknowledge their side of things, even though we can't change the outcome or fix things for them.

Only God can do that.

So we do what we can do to love them well. We show up with Jesus in our hearts and compassion in our words. And we're there, creating a sacred space where the Holy Spirit can move.

Who in your life may need this reminder today? Maybe shoot that person a quick text saying, "Hey, friend. Jesus loves you, and I love you. I'm here for you."

And if you're the person who needs to be reminded that she's a little less alone in what she's walking through right now, I'll be that friend for you in this book. I had you in mind with every word I've written and all the prayers I've prayed throughout this book. And though I don't know your specific name, God does. And He made sure our paths crossed right at this moment in your life. Sending you much love right now.

You are wondrous in how vast You are while at the same time being deeply personal and intimate. I need Your love to envelop my friend right now, and I ask for Your tender mercies to wrap all around every circumstance she is facing.

Where my wisdom falls short, I pray that my love for her reminds her that You have every answer she needs. Help her to know that all she needs to do is be obedient to You with each small step, and You will guide her way. And when she missteps, let Your loving-kindness draw her into repentance and Your grace lavish her with forgiveness.

Protect her heart and mind from the Enemy's confusion. Protect her body from being overwhelmed with strain. Bring safe people into her life and mine. And help me to be the kind of friend she needs right now.

IN JESUS' NAME,
AMEN.

PRAYER IN ACTION

Pray for the friend God brings to mind, and reach out with an invitation to spend time together. Send her a picture of this prayer so she knows she's being prayed for.

4

HOW IS FORGIVENESS EVEN POSSIBLE?

In him we have redemption through his blood, the forgiveness of sins, in accordance with the riches of God's grace that he lavished on us.

EPHESIANS 1:7–8

I wanted to obey God. But forgiveness felt so incredibly impossible with some people who had altered the course of my life with their actions. The unchangeable can feel unforgivable. There were so many betrayals, and many of the people who hurt me never owned what they did or apologized in any way. I didn't know how forgiveness would be possible when my feelings wouldn't sign on to this process.

Unforgiveness sometimes felt like the best way to protect my heart from getting hurt again.

But resentment and bitterness were turning me into someone I didn't want to be. Unforgiveness never leads to peace. And I knew that the only way to get to peace was to do what Jesus wanted me to do—forgive. Forgiveness is God's prescription to heal the hurting human heart. But I knew I would need Jesus to help me.

That's why I focus on what Jesus did on the cross and incorporate that into this process. The cross was the most holy act of forgiveness that ever took place. And it was His blood shed for our sins that was the redemptive ingredient that accomplished a forgiveness we never could have obtained or earned for ourselves.

My counselor, Jim Cress, taught me a method of dealing with forgiveness that you might want to try. He handed me a stack of three-by-five cards and told me to write on each card an action someone did that caused me pain. I placed the many cards face up all over the floor. Then Jim instructed me to say this over each card: "Out of obedience to God, I forgive ________ for _________. And whatever my feelings don't yet allow for, the blood of Jesus will surely cover it."

Then he handed me a stack of red felt squares cut slightly larger than each card. He instructed me to seal each forgiveness declaration by placing a piece of red felt over the top of the card, symbolizing the blood of Jesus and His sacrifice.

I realized that cooperating with Jesus was how I would forgive.

What a relief to know that forgiving others doesn't depend on us. We don't have to try to feel our way to forgiveness. Instead, we need to bring our willingness to forgive, not the fullness of all our restored feelings.

Forgiveness is both a decision and a process. We make the decision to forgive the facts of what happened. That's what I did that day with the cards. Now I had a marked moment to think back on to know with certainty that I had been obedient to God.

And when those bitter feelings return? Or when you get triggered with hurts from the past? You aren't a forgiveness failure. That's just evidence that you now must also walk through the process of forgiveness for the *impact* of what this hurtful situation has cost you. Take the time you need to process this impact and work through it. And then use the same script for how you've been impacted by what happened.

But remember, you deserve to stop suffering because of what someone else did to you. Forgiveness is how we find peace in the middle of hurt and betrayal.

PRAYER IN ACTION

If you feel the tug of unforgiveness in your heart, I want you to do the same forgiveness exercise my counselor had me do. Whether there is one offense or many, don't let unforgiveness live in your heart.

1. On each card, write one action someone did that caused you pain.
2. Say, "Out of obedience to God, I forgive________ for___________. And whatever my feelings don't yet allow for, the blood of Jesus will surely cover it."
3. Then seal each card by covering it with a piece of red felt or paper.

Repeat the exercise when you're triggered by the thoughts of the impact of those hurts.

Thank You for the sacrifice of Your death on the cross and Your resurrection. Because of this, I don't have to feel my way to forgiveness. I want to obey You. It's not easy, but I know that You want me to forgive. This is the way I heal. This is the way I find peace.

I place this person who hurt me into Your hands, and I trust that You will address this in Your way and in Your timing. You will handle this with equal measures of grace and justice.

Therefore, I am safe to release all my hurt and pain. I release my need to see this person punished. I release my need for an apology. I release my need for this to feel fair. I release my need for You to declare that I'm right and they're wrong. And when feelings of unforgiveness rise up, I will forgive for the impact this has had on me. Thank You for Your love, forgiveness, and peace.

IN JESUS' NAME,
AMEN.

GETTING OFF THE WELL-WORN PATH

We demolish arguments and every pretension that sets itself up against the knowledge of God, and we take captive every thought to make it obedient to Christ.

2 CORINTHIANS 10:5

Many years ago, a friend shared with me that she'd rarely heard a word of praise from either of her parents. They weren't overtly critical, yet they made it clear that she missed the mark for their standard of good. They would say things like, "Too bad you got that one bad grade on your report card; otherwise you would have been on the dean's list." What might seem like a minor comment from her parents turned into the well-worn path of *I'm not good enough* in her mind.

My friend was forty years old when she told me this, so that soundtrack had been playing in her head for a long time. And that not-good-enough story was holding her back from the hopes and dreams she had for her life—and the plans God still has for her life.

Maybe you can relate. Or maybe your soundtrack sounds more like this:

- *I fail at everything I do.*
- *If it's not perfect, it's not good at all.*
- *I'm too much!*
- *I'm such an inconvenience.*
- *I can't count on anyone else to help me or protect me.*

Today's verse tells us what to do with thoughts that hinder us from moving forward in God's purpose.

First, we demolish them. Notice how forceful those words are. When I picture a building being demolished, I picture something blowing up until it's completely gone. We need to do the same thing with lies. Remember, the Enemy wants us to forget what Jesus says about us and prevent us from glorifying Him. We have to call on the God of Angel Armies to do battle and use His strength to destroy lies.

Second, our verse says to take thoughts captive. We are thinking something at all times, so let's make sure those thoughts reflect what God thinks. If you've believed the same lie for a long time, like my friend, that lie likely created a well-worn path in your mind too. Our brains naturally take the path of least resistance, but if we replace those lies with truth from God's Word, we can create some Jesus-powered resistance that will help us get off the old path and onto the new path God has for us. We can be transformed by the renewing of our minds. We can create new paths of thinking.

PRAYER IN ACTION

Turn to the "Scriptural Prayers" section later in this book, and use them as inspiration to write your own truth-filled prayer about who God says you are.

GOD OF ANGEL ARMIES,

When I become aware of a thought that doesn't line up with Your truth, help me develop the practice of taking that thought captive to You. I want to release the lies to You in exchange for truth from Your Word.

When I think, *I'm not good enough*, remind me that "I am fearfully and wonderfully made" (Psalm 139:14). I know I have an Enemy and that the battle to believe and act on truth is a spiritual battle. So, Father, I'm asking for all Your strength and power to come against the lies of the Enemy, especially the ones I've repeated for so long.

Honestly, Lord, I'm tired of listening to that soundtrack. I'm tired of it holding me back. I don't want the hopelessness, insecurity, fear, and depression that the lies bring into my life. I want You and Your peace to rule in my heart and mind. So please help me to think in a new way. A truth-filled way.

IN JESUS' NAME, AMEN.

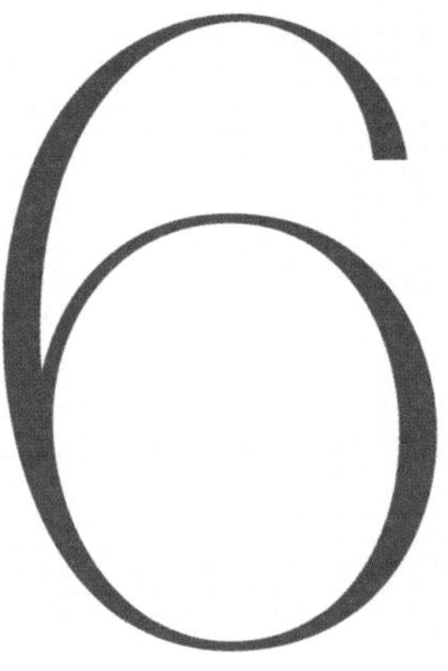

THAT'S HOW SEEDS WORK

But the Holy Spirit produces this kind of fruit in our lives: love, joy, peace, patience, kindness, goodness, faithfulness, gentleness, and self-control. There is no law against these things!

GALATIANS 5:22–23 NLT

While walking on the prayer path on my property one day, I saw a thick, swirly vine I'd never noticed before. I knew it wasn't part of the landscaping, and my curiosity was piqued. As I traced the twists and turns of its branches back through the fence, I was shocked to discover a huge, fully grown pumpkin right there in my yard. Yes, a pumpkin. That may not be unusual for you, but I don't have a garden in my yard.

I remembered that my granddaughters had been carving a pumpkin there months earlier. What I could see now was the obvious fruit of seeds that must have fallen to the ground.

I never saw the seeds, but I didn't need to. The fruit I could now see was undeniable evidence that the seeds had been there. That is simply how it works with seeds. Whatever kind of seed goes into the ground is the kind of fruit that eventually comes out of the ground.

The same is true of our hearts and lives.

When we spend consistent time with Jesus, the seed of His righteousness grows in our hearts and produces the fruit in our lives that today's verse talks about—"love, joy, peace, patience, kindness, goodness, faithfulness, gentleness, and self-control" (Galatians 5:22–23 NLT).

The fruit of the Spirit is evidence of God's Spirit in us. It does not mean we're perfect, but it does mean that more and more often, in the way we treat others, we will notice these things:

Love replaces selfishness.
Joy replaces angry outbursts and edgy frustration.
Peace replaces demands for control.
Patience replaces a quick temper.
Kindness replaces rudeness.
Goodness replaces selfish ambition.

Faithfulness replaces incessant desire for self-gratification.
Gentleness replaces a harsh approach.
Self-control replaces unrestrained impulses.

Growth takes time. Be patient with yourself and consistent with God. It's about progress, not perfection. Those pumpkin seeds had been in the ground nearly ninety days before I saw their fruit. I love knowing that God made us full of potential and purpose. We can trust that He made us to produce fruit. Good fruit. Fruit that brings glory to Him.

Apart from God, we can do nothing. Just like that pumpkin could not have grown without the seeds the girls dropped, the fruit of the Spirit cannot grow unless we choose to spend time talking to Jesus and filling our hearts and minds with the good seeds of God's Word.

PRAYER IN ACTION

Be on the lookout for ways you're growing. And when you see the signs of new fruit springing up, encourage yourself. You *are* making progress, and God sees it too. Thank Him for the work He's doing in your heart.

DEAR LORD,

I don't want to just know You; I want the fruit of my life to reflect You in all I say and do. Help me to show Your love, joy, peace, patience, kindness, goodness, faithfulness, gentleness, and self-control to everyone I encounter.

Thank You for loving me just as I am, but help me recognize the areas where I need more growth.

Help me to rest in Your timing and trust that as I spend time with You, I will be transformed.

Lord, I pray that more and more of You will flow through me so that when others see me, they will see more of You. Give me the strength to keep pressing into Your presence even when I don't feel like I'm making progress. I trust that You are faithful to complete the good work You started in me.

IN JESUS' NAME,
AMEN.

YOU MAY NOT HAVE ALL THE EVIDENCE

Let your gentleness be evident to all.

PHILIPPIANS 4:5

Judgments cast. Assumptions made. Blame assigned. Labels given.

It's so easy to cast judgment, whether we simply think the words or actually say them aloud.

Your coworker with that annoying habit. Your friend who always seems to be complaining about something. The woman at Bible study who never seems to engage. Or the one who engages too much. That stranger in the grocery store whose child is screaming. The neighbor who always seems grumpy.

Would your thoughts change if you knew that the person you feel so annoyed with was processing some kind of pain you didn't know about? Or if you knew they were trying to figure out something really complicated and emotional in their life?

Chances are, they are facing or have faced a daunting challenge. How do I know? Because they're humans living in the same confusing, chaotic, and hard-to-understand world that often breaks your heart and mine. We don't have to know all the details of their story to offer what they need most: gentleness instead of judgment. It's the same thing you and I need most days.

The gentleness of grace sounds like, "That must be frustrating," or, "Is there something I can do to support you?" It looks like a kind text sent or grocery store flowers left at the front door. It can even be something as simple as a smile.

Let's choose gentleness. Let's choose kindness. Let's choose understanding. Let's choose grace.

Instead of our first reaction being to label that person based on what she's *doing* right now, let's pray for her based on what she might be *facing* right now. Let's help the ones God places right in front of us. Judgment can end with us when we let the gentleness of God flow through us.

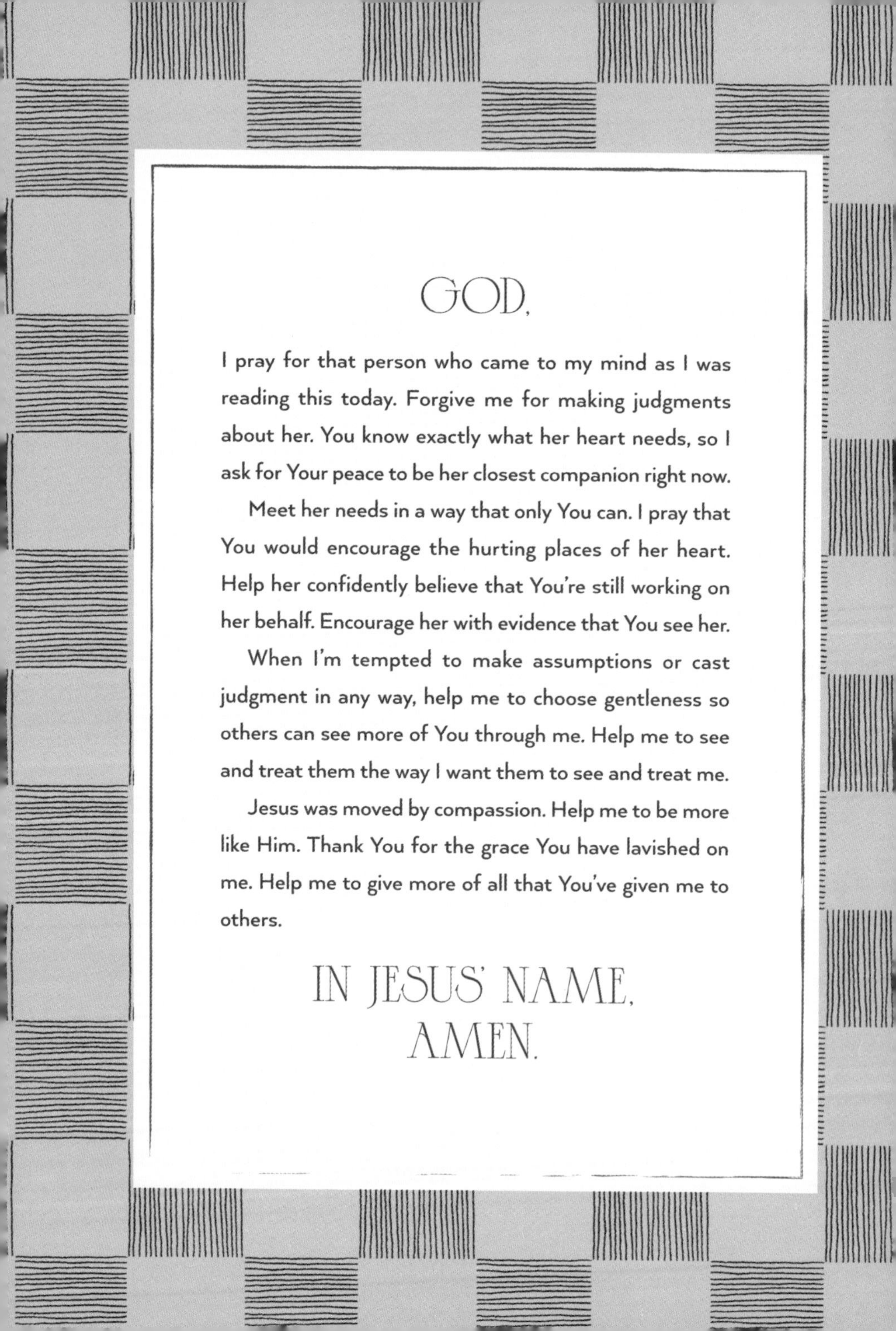

GOD,

I pray for that person who came to my mind as I was reading this today. Forgive me for making judgments about her. You know exactly what her heart needs, so I ask for Your peace to be her closest companion right now.

Meet her needs in a way that only You can. I pray that You would encourage the hurting places of her heart. Help her confidently believe that You're still working on her behalf. Encourage her with evidence that You see her.

When I'm tempted to make assumptions or cast judgment in any way, help me to choose gentleness so others can see more of You through me. Help me to see and treat them the way I want them to see and treat me.

Jesus was moved by compassion. Help me to be more like Him. Thank You for the grace You have lavished on me. Help me to give more of all that You've given me to others.

IN JESUS' NAME,
AMEN.

PRAYER IN ACTION

As you go about your day, ask the Lord to show you the right gesture that will let His gentleness flow through you to that person you're tempted to judge. It can be as simple as a text. Trust the Lord to show you.

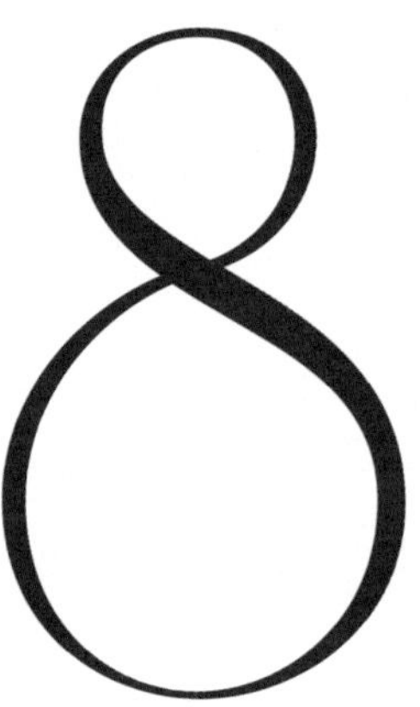

THE GRABBINESS OF OUR FLESH

And I pray that you, being rooted and established in love, may have power, together with all the Lord's holy people, to grasp how wide and long and high and deep is the love of Christ.

EPHESIANS 3:17–18

I don't like to be in pain. And if I'm not careful, this aversion to pain can lead to me grabbing at anyone and anything to fill the deep ache in my soul. Maybe you can relate.

When you're lonely and you see your friends post a picture together at a gathering you weren't invited to, your flesh will want to grab at something. It's hard not to comfort yourself by venting all your frustrations to another friend or family member. When you're listening to another mom talk about the great job her adult child got but yours can't find his direction, your flesh will want to grab at something. It's hard not to throw out a statement to one-up the bragging moms in an area where your child is excelling.

These things we're tempted to grab won't fill us the way we hope. In the end, they only make us feel emptier. But how do we tell our flesh "no" when we are desperate for relief? I've discovered that the more we fill ourselves with Christ's life-giving love, the less we will give into the grabbiness of our flesh.

One of the most beautiful descriptions of the fullness of God is found in Paul's prayer in Ephesians we read today. My favorite part of this prayer is Paul's request that we will have the power to grasp the fullness of the love of Christ. If we do this, we'll be more and more grounded in God's love. And we won't grab at other things to fill us. Or if we do, we'll sense our error. We'll feel a prick in our spirits when our flesh makes frenzied swipes at satisfaction, and we'll pause.

So we have a daily choice: Am I willing to tell my flesh "no" so I can say "yes" to the fullness of God?

We have the power through Christ, who is over every power, including the pull of the flesh. When we have Christ, we are full—fully loved and accepted and empowered to say no.

This is true on the days when we feel Jesus' love, and it's still true on the days when we don't feel it.

If we live rooted and established in His love, we don't just have knowledge of His love in our minds, but it becomes a reality that anchors us. Though winds of hurt or disappointment or fear blow, they cannot uproot us and rip us apart. God's love holds us. His love grounds us. His love fills us.

PRAYER IN ACTION

When you feel like saying yes to your flesh, redirect yourself to Jesus by listening to worship music, singing praises, praying, or texting a friend to pray for you.

Help me to grasp how deep Your love is for me, and let Your love fill me and satisfy me. As I read Your Word, pray, and worship, may my roots grow down deeper in Your love.

Open my eyes so that I see the places where I've tried to fill myself up with the desires and pull of the flesh instead of You.

Sometimes when I'm hurting, lonely, mad, or scared, I reach for what I mistakenly think will take away the pain. Maybe it's an indulgence, a habit, a sin pattern. I don't want to do this anymore. I want to reach for You. Each time I do this, I am more established and anchored in Your love. Help me look to You and You alone to fill me.

IN YOUR NAME,
AMEN.

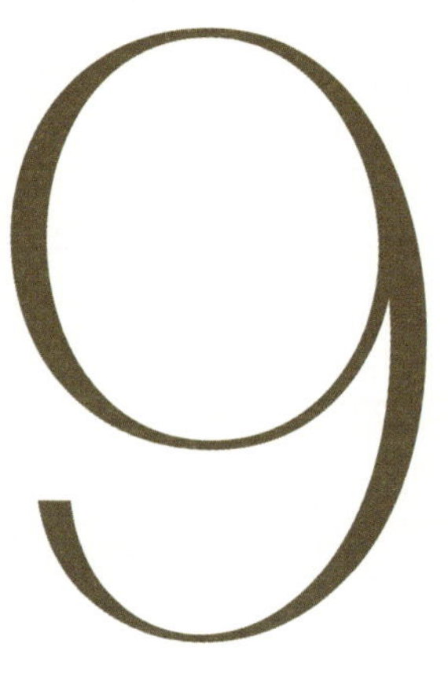

A PRAYER OF DECLARATION: PRAISING GOD FOR WHO HE IS

Today you'll find a prayer of declaration. Think of it as an announcement of truth to remind yourself and the Enemy of the truth God speaks over your life. Scattered throughout the remainder of the book you'll find declarations filled with biblical truth to seal into your heart what you've been learning.

These declarations help align our hearts, minds, and steps with His will and His ways. They push back the Enemy by boldly proclaiming not only our faith in God but also our trust that He is at work in our lives.

Today's declaration is one of praise, reminding you and me exactly who God is. It's based on the following Scripture:

> *"Yours, Lord, is the greatness and the power*
> *and the glory and the majesty and the splendor,*
> *for everything in heaven and earth is yours.*
> *Yours, Lord, is the kingdom;*
> *you are exalted as head over all."*
>
> 1 CHRONICLES 29:11

LORD, YOU ARE MY SAVIOR.

You are the source of forgiveness, mercy, grace, and salvation. In You I find redemption, new life, and love beyond measure.

Lord, You are my King of kings and Lord of lords. You reign above all. You are sovereign and mighty. Your power and authority are unmatched. My knees and heart bow to acknowledge how great You are.

Lord, You are my Rock, my firm foundation in times of uncertainty, doubt, and confusion. You are steady ground when chaos is close to me and in the world around me. I won't be shaken.

Lord, You are my Comforter, the Lifter of my head. You know my sadness and have kept track of my tears. You replace my anxiety, depression, grief, and troubled heart with Your comfort and peace.

You are my Healer, restoring my body, mind, heart, and spirit. I am no longer broken, weary, downtrodden, hopeless, or discouraged. I have new life in You.

You are my Shepherd. You lead me beside still waters, where my soul is refreshed and restored. I can trust where You lead, even if I don't understand the direction of the path.

Lord, You alone are worthy of my praise. I place You above all, in all, around all. And I trust You with it all.

IN JESUS' NAME, AMEN!

PRAYER IN ACTION

Which part of today's declaration spoke most personally to you? Write that (or the whole declaration) on a piece of paper and put it in a place you'll see throughout your day. Speak it to yourself or aloud every time you see it or it comes to mind. You can even send it to a friend who could use these truths today.

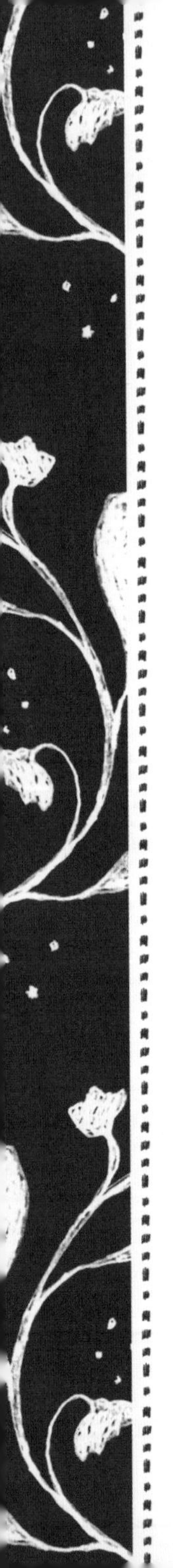

A LETTER FROM LYSA

DEAR FRIEND,

If you're feeling a bit off today, remember Psalm 37:4, where we are instructed to "take delight in the LORD, and he will give you the desires of your heart." Sometimes I want to rush to what He will give me rather than what I'm supposed to do first—which is to delight in Him. And I feel challenged to change this.

Often I come to the Lord with my stresses and hardships and confusion. But I'm encouraged by this verse to also come to Him with my delight in who He is, how faithful He is, how good He is, and how much I love Him.

Something in my heart shifts in such a good way when I'm listening to praise music. So I wonder if that same thing might happen when I praise Him first in my prayers with expressions of my delight in Him.

Then, the more I delight in Him, the more my heart will align with His heart. And then my desires become more about pleasing Him and less and less about pleasing myself.

I don't want to get tricked by the Enemy and believe the lie that things in this world will give me anything close to what my heart really longs for. I want my heart to be a pure reflection of God's lasting joy, His peace, His kindness, and His love.

GUIDED BY HIS WORD, NOT MY EVER-CHANGING EMOTIONS

Come near to God and he will come near to you.

JAMES 4:8

Sometimes we know things to be true with our heads, but our hearts need more reassurance. When life feels really hard, we need the reminder that God promises His presence, His protection, and His provision for whatever comes our way.

I needed those reminders more than ever during the hard years of dealing with betrayal in my marriage. My ever-changing emotions were guiding me to all the wrong places. Places like despair and anger. I desperately needed a way to draw near to God and push back the thoughts and fears about my family's rearranged future and the desire to sink down into the comfort of my bed to avoid it all.

I can't physically see God, so the best way I know to draw near to Him is by getting in His Word, allowing Him to reframe my perspective, and letting His truth comfort and fill the hurting places in my mind and heart.

I have learned to protect my time with Jesus by being purposeful with my morning hours. I know it is crucial to first fill my mind with His Word before the demands of a busy schedule, people who need my attention, or a phone that begs me to scroll.

I know the Bible is a beautiful melody of God's truth. So even on the days when I don't quite feel its song rising off the pages, I can trust that His Word is doing the work in my heart that God intends. My job is to commit my heart to God and seek Him first in all things. His job is everything else.

His Word will arm us with truth to fight whatever causes us to doubt His goodness, rob us of peace, or cause us anxiety. If we choose to be intentional with the time we spend in God's Word, it can become a blanket of love and comfort surrounding us, filling us with gratitude, and preparing us for the day.

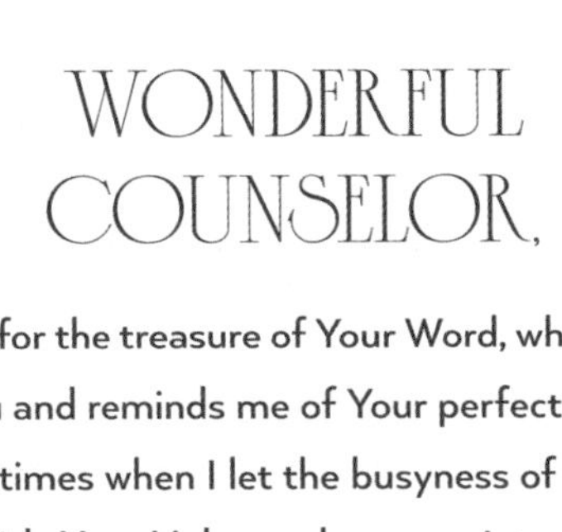

WONDERFUL COUNSELOR,

Thank You for the treasure of Your Word, which draws me near to You and reminds me of Your perfect love. Forgive me for the times when I let the busyness of the day steal my time with You. Help me be more intentional about seeking You first each morning.

I know that You desire to give me just what I need for today's assignments. Time with You settles my soul and shifts my perspective.

Help me walk by Your Word, not my feelings. Give me Your wisdom, counsel, and peace. Protect me from my own careless thoughts, words, and actions. And keep me from being distracted by how I think things should be.

IN JESUS' NAME, AMEN.

PRAYER IN ACTION

Make a new commitment to spend time reading God's Word and praying daily. If you miss the time you had planned, remember that He's always available and you can open His Word any time of day.

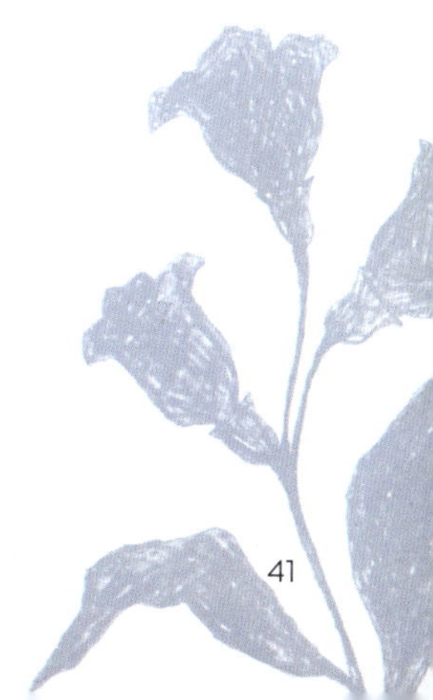

11

SMALL COMPROMISES, BIG CONSEQUENCES

Above all else, guard your heart,
for everything you do flows from it.

PROVERBS 4:23

Have you ever been tempted to make seemingly small compromises in the short-term that had the potential to take you away from God's best in the long-term? Small compromises can build on one another until they become a mountain of regret.

Temptation of any kind is Satan's invitation to have our needs met outside the will of God. Satan wants to plant seeds of doubt in our minds, causing us to question if God can and will satisfy our needs.

Satan's temptations can be so subtle that they don't seem like temptations at all. Indulging in those couple of glasses of wine each night or bingeing on that pint of ice cream. Watching shows that are just a bit risqué. Maybe it's the Amazon purchases you can't quite afford. Or the slightly flirtatious text you send to a coworker.

And that leads to half-truths, excuses, justifications, and secrets. *It's just a small thing to look forward to. I didn't tell anyone because it's not a big deal. Everyone I know does it. I've been working so hard that I deserve this. It's not really sin, is it?*

Are these examples always sin? Not necessarily. That's why God tells us that guarding our hearts is so important. It means getting honest with ourselves by asking deeper questions like, *Is this thought, desire, or behavior distancing me from God or drawing me closer to Him?*

Guarding our hearts also means asking God to help us determine what should go into our hearts and choosing to fill our lives with things that draw us closer to Him. Things like spending time with other Christians, setting aside time for God, studying His Word, and praying continuously.

Scripture tells us to be on the alert, reminding us that Satan is always looking for ways to deceive us because he is the Father of Lies (John 8:44). And if we aren't watchful, Satan's temptations will cause us to make small compromises today that could turn into big consequences later.

LORD,

Sometimes what I long for and think I need seems so unattainable that I just want what feels good now. But I want to make choices that lead me closer to You. I don't want to trade Your best for what temporarily fills me today. I confess that I get weary and weak in the waiting, and that makes me vulnerable to the lies of the Enemy.

Teach me how to guard my heart. Help me recognize the small compromises I'm making that distance me from You. Forgive me for them. Give me the strength to resist them and make better choices.

I want all my thoughts, desires, and behaviors to honor and please You above all else. Fill my mind with Your truth and my heart with Your love. Thank You that your grace is sufficient, and Your strength is made perfect in my weakness.

You promise to meet all my needs. Help me trust in Your provision alone. I know You're not holding out on me. Instead, You're holding on to me with love. You created me and You know what's best for me. Help me believe this wholeheartedly.

IN JESUS' NAME, AMEN.

PRAYER IN ACTION

Decide to be on the alert today, and let God show you where you've made small compromises. As He brings those things to your mind throughout the day, repent where necessary and thank Him for helping you guard your heart.

12

HANDPICKED

"I am the Lord's servant," Mary answered.

"May your word to me be fulfilled."

LUKE 1:38

Do you ever find yourself scrolling on social media, imagining the lives of all the put-together people who seem perfectly suited for all their roles while you're struggling? Thinking maybe God should have picked someone else? Wondering if there is more to life than just the mundane tasks of each day?

I remember a time when I begged God to make me just like this supermom I heard speak at a parenting seminar. Why couldn't I be more like her? My days seemed disorganized and chaotic. What was wrong with me? I felt so unqualified that I mentally beat myself up for not having what it took to be a great mom.

Then one day in Bible study, I read the story of Mary, the teenage mother of Jesus. And I realized that she didn't meet the new supermom standard I'd set for myself.

Somehow, Mary—simple, ordinary, and perhaps quite common—had been handpicked by God to be Jesus' mother. And the only qualification she seemed to have was a willing heart.

It's easy to let my thoughts drift, tempting me to rattle off a list of all the reasons I'm not enough. Maybe you can relate. That's why Mary's story helped me so much. Today's verse reveals that Mary's trust was not in her own abilities but in the One who chose her for the role.

All God wanted from Mary was her willingness. And that's all He wants from you and me too. He has already given you the exact qualities you need for your roles—as a mother, wife, daughter, sister, employee, neighbor, business owner, or friend.

So whatever has you feeling ordinary and listing all the things that make you unqualified, I want you to know that God loves to take ordinary people just like you and me and do extraordinary things in them, through them, and with them.

I'm grateful that You don't look at the outward appearance but rather You see my heart. Like Mary, I offer You my willingness, trusting that You have handpicked me for the assignments You have given me.

Forgive me for letting the negative thoughts I have about myself diminish the way You created me. I know that everything You allow in my life is shaping and preparing me for the purpose You have for me.

Thank You for reminding me that what is impossible with me is possible with You.

IN JESUS' NAME,
AMEN.

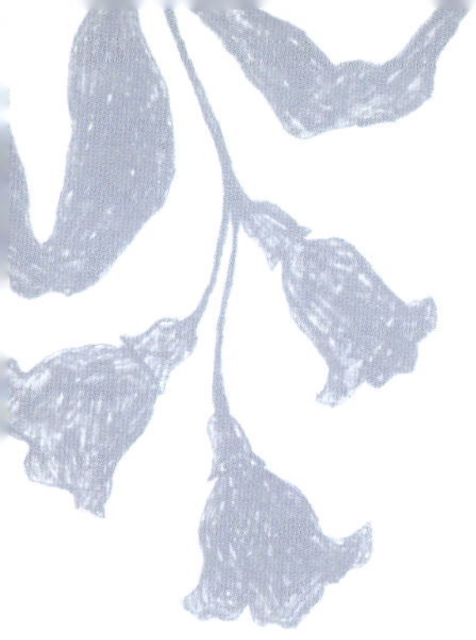

PRAYER IN ACTION

Take a single ordinary flower from your yard, and place it in a vase. Each time you see it, remind yourself, *I'm handpicked by God.*

13

HARD TIMES CAN BE HOLY TIMES

"I have told you these things, so that in me you may have peace. In this world you will have trouble. But take heart! I have overcome the world."

JOHN 16:33

Sometimes we think if we can just get through this circumstance, life will finally be calm. We'll at last have the peace and happiness we've longed for. But what if life settling down and all your disappointments going away was the worst thing that could happen to you? What if your "I don't know" is helping you grow in trusting Jesus?

When we're scared, uncomfortable, confused, or struggling with a situation, it's so easy to focus on simply wanting the pain to go away and to finally be free of challenges and struggles. We long for relief and comfort and peace. And we can have those things—but not by focusing on all our problems being gone. As today's verse reminds us, our hearts must stay close to Him by trusting in His promise to overcome.

I wish I could promise you that your struggles will soon go away or that everything will turn out just the way you want it to. Yet as much as I wish I could, I can't. What I can promise you is this: Challenges can help us learn to depend on God.

Depending on Him means we keep praying, we keep believing, we keep trusting His promises. We can't see the whole picture right now, but God does. And relying on Him means we trust that there is a reason why He isn't letting us see the whole picture. Maybe if we knew too much, we would rush past the lessons God has for us that are crucially important for our futures. The training ground is here in the "I don't know." This time isn't a waste, and it's definitely not pointless when we are walking with God.

Let's cry out to God, declaring that this hard time will be a holy time, a close-to-God time. And let's choose to believe that, even in these places, good is happening. Because wherever God is, good is always working.

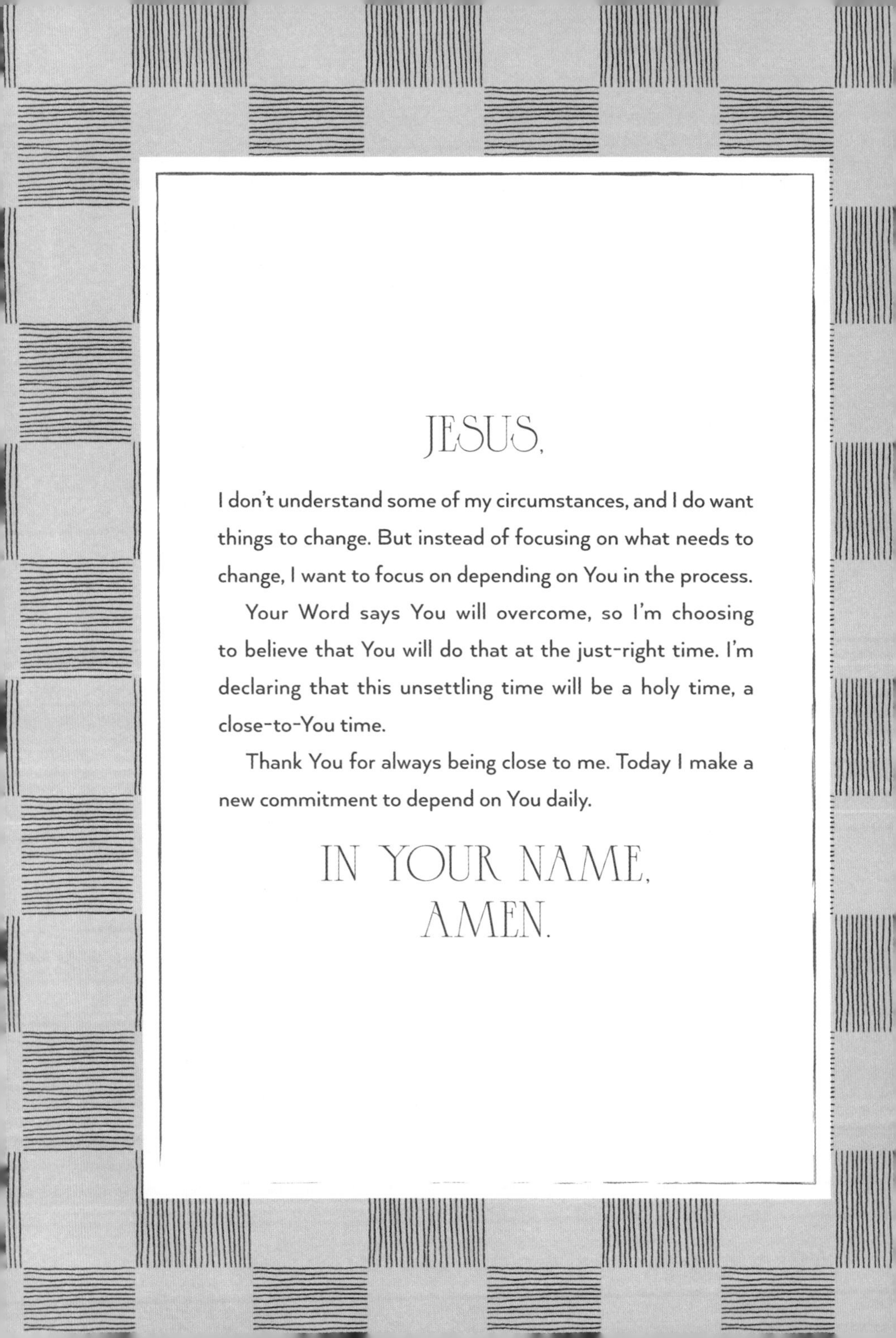

JESUS,

I don't understand some of my circumstances, and I do want things to change. But instead of focusing on what needs to change, I want to focus on depending on You in the process.

Your Word says You will overcome, so I'm choosing to believe that You will do that at the just-right time. I'm declaring that this unsettling time will be a holy time, a close-to-You time.

Thank You for always being close to me. Today I make a new commitment to depend on You daily.

IN YOUR NAME,
AMEN.

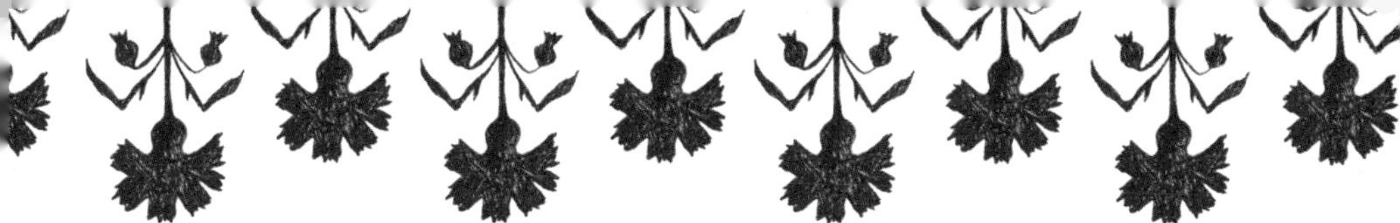

PRAYER IN ACTION

Today when your heart cries out for that hard thing to change, instead whisper to Jesus, "Thank You, Lord, for being close."

THE PLACE WORRY CAN'T REACH ME

Praise him, sun and moon! Praise him, all you twinkling stars! Praise him, skies above! Praise him, vapors high above the clouds! Let every created thing give praise to the LORD, for he issued his command, and they came into being.

PSALM 148:3–5 NLT

Sometimes my soul just needs a song. Something in me shifts when praise music is on. That's not just a feeling. Praising God's name actually ushers God's presence into even the darkest of moments.

Praise reminds our souls how near God is and how good He is. It lifts our thoughts to a place where the worries of this world can no longer reach us.

Anytime we feel stuck in a place of wanting something about our lives to be different—when anxiety and worry overwhelm our thoughts or we get the sinking feeling that we're missing out or being overlooked, when we sense a deep hunger or thirst that doesn't ever seem to be quenched—I believe our souls are crying out for us to worship God. Really worship Him.

And I don't mean simply repeating words on a screen in a sanctuary on Sunday. Or clapping when we're supposed to clap. We were made for more than to simply follow, repeat, and tap our toes to the beat. Sometimes we need to remind ourselves what today's verse explains: Along with all creation, you and I were literally created to worship our Creator. To tell Him how much we love Him. To thank Him for His goodness. To sing our own songs of praise to Him.

And when we do, He promises to bring all of Himself to us. That means:

His love
His peace
His kindness
His joy
His truth
His security
His faithfulness

No matter what this day holds, choose to worship your way through it, letting your expression of love toward God flow out of you as a song of praise to Him. Not for what He does but for who He is.

PRAYER IN ACTION

Let's try a posture of praise today. Slip out your back door, step into the sunlight, and look toward the sky. As you feel the warmth of the sun's rays on your face, lift your hands up and say, "If all creation sings Your praises, so will I!"

CREATOR OF THE UNIVERSE,

I cry out from the deep places where I feel dried up and hollow. You are the only One who can fill me. Forgive me for not making praise a habit.

You are worthy of all praise. And today I choose to worship You with my whole being. I lift my hands to the heavens and join the angels in singing, "Holy, holy, holy is the Lord God Almighty" (Revelation 4:8).

I want my life to be a sacrifice of praise to You. Thank You for creating me. Thank You for loving me. I love You, Lord.

IN JESUS' NAME, AMEN.

I HAVE DECIDED

I sought the L*ORD*, *and he answered me;*
he delivered me from all my fears.

PSALM 34:4

When I surveyed people and asked, "What do you think is the biggest reason people struggle to make decisions?" overwhelmingly, the answer was fear. Fear of the unknown. Fear of getting hurt. Fear of what others will think. Fear of making the wrong decision.

Having fear is normal. Wrestling with fear is normal. But we shouldn't let fear become so big that it paralyzes us. When we do, we end up stuck.

I wish it weren't so, but we live in a fallen, broken world, which means there is no choice that will turn out perfectly. But if fear has you spinning in circles today, I've got some truths that will help calm your heart, bring more clarity to the process, and help get you moving again:

1. Our perfect God will be with you no matter where your decision takes you (Psalm 139:8).
2. God is the best rerouter (Isaiah 30:21).
3. No decision is irredeemable (Joel 2:25).
4. Nothing is too big for God (Jeremiah 32:17).
5. Contrary to how it may feel, your life probably does not depend on this decision (Psalm 139:16; Isaiah 46:10).
6. God is always working, even when we can't see it (John 5:17; Romans 8:28).
7. His love for you will not change regardless of your decision (Psalm 100:5; Romans 8:38–39).

I know this decision feels heavy, and I don't have all the answers you need. But I can tell you this: Deciding to turn your eyes to Jesus and trusting Him with the outcome is always a wise decision.

I confess that I've let fear paralyze me. Forgive me for thinking that I can control the outcomes in my life.

Thank You for the comfort of Your Word. Today I decide to place my trust in You, knowing that no matter what the outcome of this decision is, You will be with me to provide whatever I need.

I release control. I release the fear of making a wrong decision.

I turn my eyes to You. Please tune my ears to hear Your instructions, telling me which way to go. Help me recognize Your answers to my prayers. Reveal Yourself to me, Lord.

IN JESUS' NAME,
AMEN.

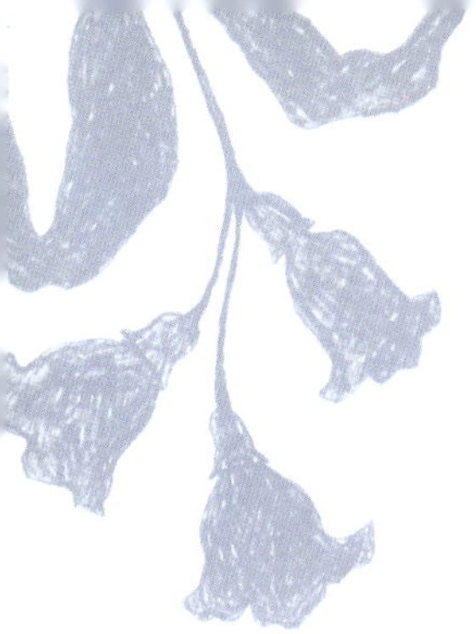

PRAYER IN ACTION

There's an old song called "I Have Decided to Follow Jesus." If you don't know it, take a second to look it up. And every time one of those fears about the decision you're facing pops up today, start quietly humming that song: "I have decided to follow Jesus, no turning back, no turning back." Not only will the lyrics remind you where to place your trust, but here's a fun fact: Humming stimulates our vagus nerve, which helps calm anxiety.

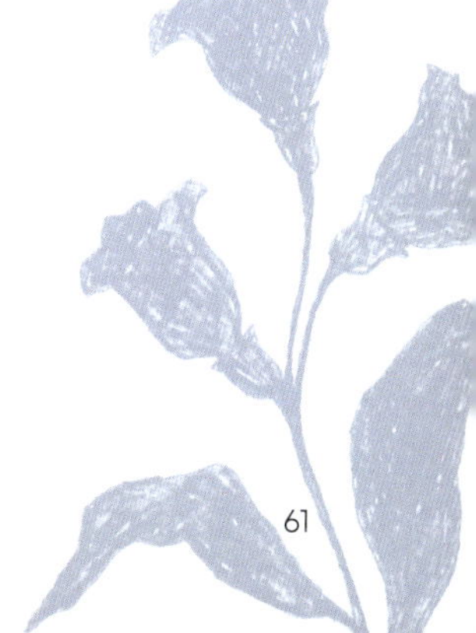

QUIETLY QUITTING ON HOPE

May the God of hope fill you with all joy and peace as you trust in him, so that you may overflow with hope by the power of the Holy Spirit.

ROMANS 15:13

For me, hope either ushers in the most beautiful feeling of possibility or a dreaded feeling that I probably won't get what I keep praying for. But if we're not willing to risk hoping, then we're already quietly quitting on a better future.

There have been times when I really believed God's answer would line up with what I prayed for. But that wasn't what happened, so quitting on hope seemed like the only reasonable choice to make. It felt like the best way to protect my heart from the ache of another unanswered prayer. So I get it. Hope itself can feel like the most brutal risk of all.

But if we limit our view of life to the hardships of today, we'll trade dreaming for dread. We'll exchange looking forward with joy for looking backward with sorrow. We'll swap the anticipation of future possibilities for the angst of staying stuck in the pain of right now.

When we quit on hope, we become blind to the evidence of God's goodness all around us. And if we lose sight of God's goodness, trusting Him and hoping in Him will feel foolish. It's difficult to keep trusting God when it feels like He's letting us down.

Maybe you've been there.

Have prayers that seemed to go unanswered allowed your thoughts to fill with worst-case scenarios and tempted you to stop hoping altogether?

I want to challenge you to stop feeding those anxious thoughts and to say out loud, "But what if it does all work out?" Pause and let that new question have some space in your mind.

And now start fueling that spark of hope by recounting the many everyday moments when God has come through for you—when things did work out. For example, "My kids are thriving in school" or "My body was healthy enough to do all that I did today." These are evidence that, more times than not, things really do work out okay. And we can choose to let those moments fuel our hope for today, and then again for tomorrow.

This isn't denying that hard things still happen, and it's not denying the reality that things may not work out like we hope. But it's choosing to remember all that actually is working out. It's choosing to see God's goodness in the midst of the hard and allowing that to balance our thoughts so we can continue to believe in a future that contains good possibilities. God possibilities.

PRAYER IN ACTION

As soon as you sense those worst-case scenario thoughts filling your mind, stop and say, "But what if it does work out?" Then pause again and notice how that new question shifts your perspective.

LORD JESUS,

Scripture tells me that hope comes from You, "the God of hope," so that's where I'm turning my thoughts in this hard-to-understand place.

I want to keep hope alive in my heart, so I'm choosing to let go of my catastrophic thinking. I'm giving *What if it does work out?* the space it needs to grow.

Remind me of all the times when things did work out, all the times You have come through for me. Help me to keep having courage, to keep opening my heart to the possibilities of a better future, and to give myself grace in the process.

I want to see the evidence of Your goodness around me. And help me to remember that ultimately my hope is in You. Thank You for the promise of joy and peace as I trust *You*.

IN YOUR NAME,
AMEN.

17

A PRAYER OF DECLARATION: I AM SAFE WITH YOU

Nothing makes me forget who God is more than fear. And fear comes in all kinds of forms—anxiety, doubt, dread, and panic. It can paralyze us. It can immobilize our faith. It can cause us to grasp for control. And it can lead to tunnel vision where we see only our circumstances, not God. Maybe you can relate to one of these reactions right now.

When I'm caught up in fear, I desperately want to feel safe.

So the promise found in today's scripture means so much to me, and I hope it will to you too. God is our safe place. Always. And for every situation.

Let today's scripture and declaration remind you to run to Him for safety, shelter, and security.

> *He who takes refuge in the shelter of the Most High will be* safe *in the shadow of the Almighty. He will say to the Eternal, "My shelter, my* mighty *fortress, my God, I place* all *my trust in You." For He will rescue you from the snares set by your enemies* who entrap you *and from deadly plagues.* Like a bird protecting its young, *God will cover you with His feathers, will protect you under His* great *wings; His faithfulness will form a shield around you, a rock-solid wall* to protect you.
>
> PSALM 91:1–4 The Voice

LORD, I AM SAFE WITH YOU.

I proclaim out loud, "You are 'my shelter, my *mighty* fortress, my God, I place *all* my trust in You'" (Psalm 91:2 THE VOICE).

You comfort me and calm my fear of unknowns and uncertainties.

You are my fortress, a strong, high place. It's the place You lift me so fear can no longer have access to me. Fear can't stop what it can no longer reach. What a comfort this is. You lift me high when I lift my soul and worship Your holy name.

With You, Lord, I'm not afraid. You are my quick place to duck into when fear nips at the edges of my emotions. I close my eyes and proclaim out loud that You are my safe place!

I remind the Enemy that I will not entertain his whispered lies. The lies that tell me I will always be alone and lonely and that I will always be afraid. Not today. Not tomorrow. Not ever.

You are my shelter. Under Your protection, I can rest. You are my sentry. You command Your angels to watch over me.

Lord, in You I have security. Security that is not dependent on a person or a situation. I am secure because I can call on You anytime fear rises up, and I can trust that You will answer.

You will fight for me. You will help me avoid the snares and traps of the Enemy of my soul. And You will trample the lions and serpents that threaten my life. Nothing has more power than You.

Yes, Lord, I declare that I am safe with You.

IN JESUS' NAME, AMEN.

PRAYER IN ACTION

Which part of today's declaration spoke most personally to you? Write that (or the whole declaration) on a piece of paper and put it in a place you'll see throughout your day. Speak it to yourself or aloud every time you see it or it comes to mind. You can even send it to a friend who could use these truths today.

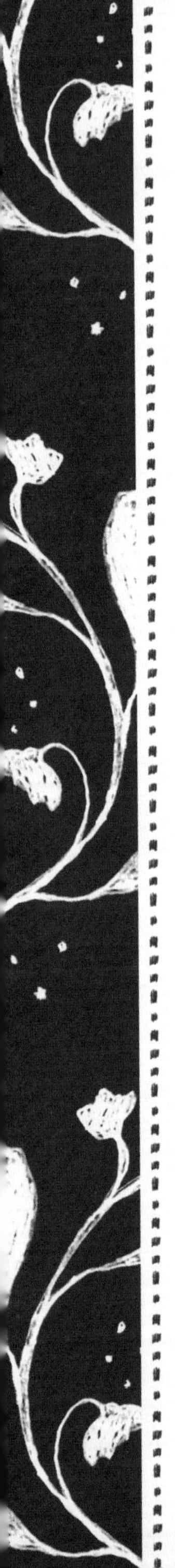

A LETTER FROM LYSA

DEAR FRIEND,

Remember the practice I shared when we started our journey at the beginning of this book? The one I started more than twenty years ago of intentionally looking for evidence of God's reality throughout my day? I want to encourage you with that today: God's activity is how God answers prayers. Probably not all the answers you want. But that activity in the everyday reminds us that His answers are still in process.

I used to feel a boost only when I saw Him answer one of the big prayers, but noticing the everyday evidence of His presence helps me remember that He is still working on the answers. The answers that will be best for me and everyone involved. It helps me remember that God is never silent. He is always at work.

God loves us too much to answer our prayers in any other way than the right way. And He loves us too much to answer our prayers in any other timing than the right timing. So if you have been discouraged because you don't sense God answering like you thought He would, look for His faithfulness and goodness in some other way today. And know that the goodness you see is part of God's answer that is still on the way, reminding you that He is with you and will never leave you.

WE DO NOT SERVE A DO-NOTHING GOD

Casting all your cares [all your anxieties, all your worries, and all your concerns, once and for all] on Him, for He cares about you [with deepest affection, and watches over you very carefully].

1 PETER 5:7 AMP

If you're desperate for God's intervention in your story, oh friend, I understand. I can't give you a save-the-date of when to expect the breakthrough, but I can remind you of God's faithfulness with the wisdom I've learned in my own life. Don't think for one minute that God isn't doing something.

We don't serve a do-nothing God. He is always working.

The story of Joseph in the book of Genesis is a good reminder of this. Joseph walked through years of hardships—betrayed by his family, sold into slavery, falsely accused, thrown into prison. He was seemingly forgotten . . . but with God, there is always a "meanwhile." God was bringing about something only He could do with Joseph's life. He was positioning Joseph and preparing him to help save the lives of millions of people during a famine that would have otherwise destroyed them.

On this side of eternity we don't always get to see how God is working in our most painful situations. But we can let the way God worked in Joseph's story remind us that even when we can't see it, God is always doing something.

I look back at times in my life when I wondered if I'd survive the situations I was facing, and confidently say, *There was never one moment when God was doing nothing.*

Sometimes it can feel like God is absent, but remember, as today's verse says, He is watching over you carefully. So keep casting your cares on Him, and keep reminding yourself that He's working even when you can't see it, because you do not serve a do-nothing God.

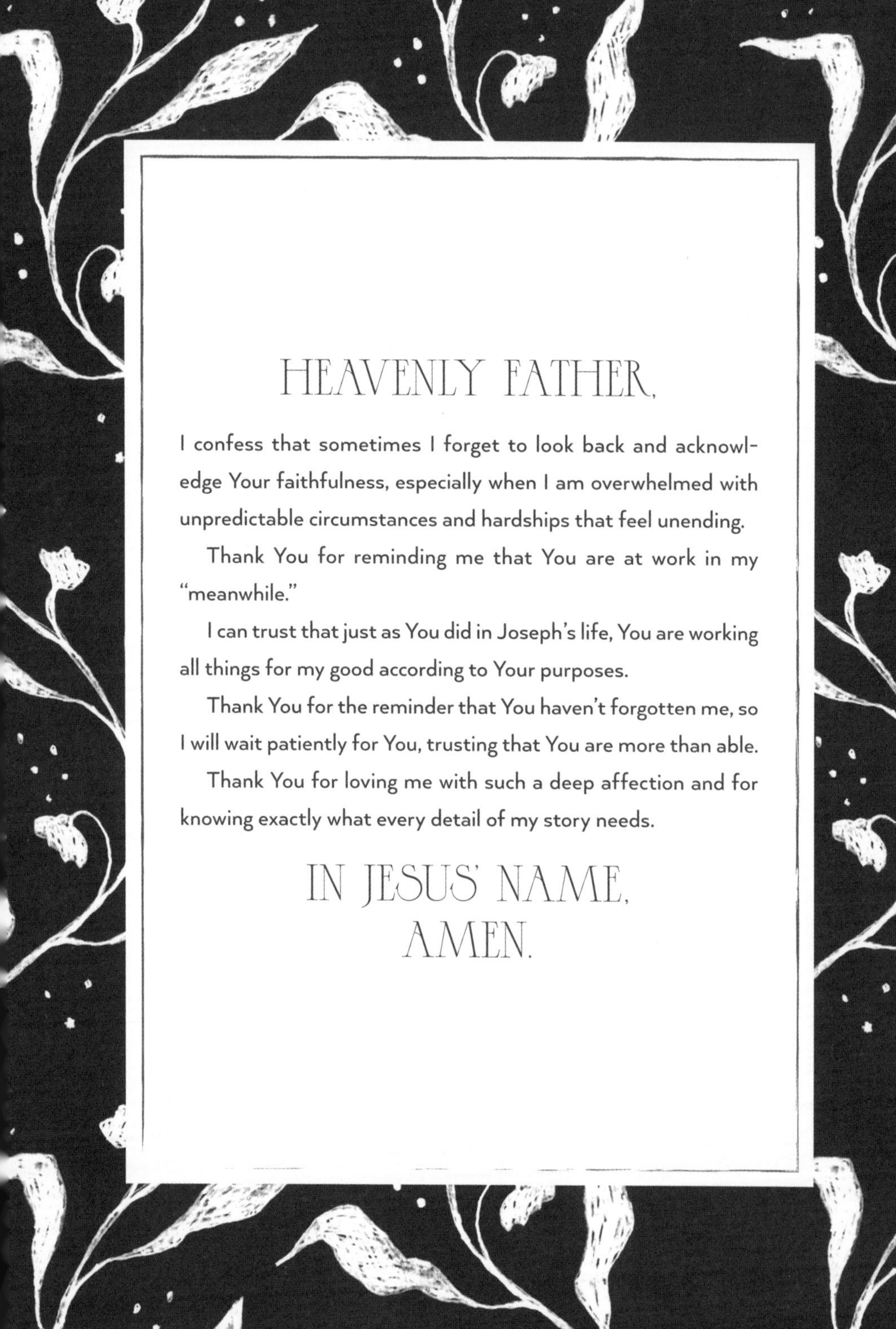

HEAVENLY FATHER,

I confess that sometimes I forget to look back and acknowledge Your faithfulness, especially when I am overwhelmed with unpredictable circumstances and hardships that feel unending.

Thank You for reminding me that You are at work in my "meanwhile."

I can trust that just as You did in Joseph's life, You are working all things for my good according to Your purposes.

Thank You for the reminder that You haven't forgotten me, so I will wait patiently for You, trusting that You are more than able.

Thank You for loving me with such a deep affection and for knowing exactly what every detail of my story needs.

IN JESUS' NAME,
AMEN.

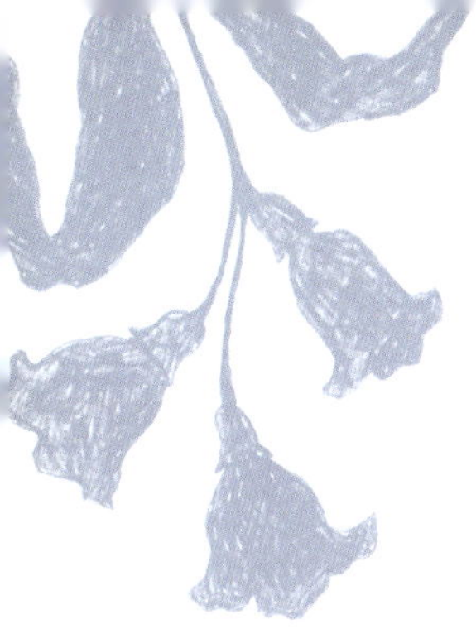

PRAYER IN ACTION

When you start to feel frustrated or to despair about what feels like repeated unanswered prayer, remind yourself, *I do not serve a do-nothing God. He is always working.*

COMPLETELY SURRENDERED

When Jesus heard this, he said to him, "You still lack one thing. Sell everything you have and give to the poor, and you will have treasure in heaven. Then come, follow me."

LUKE 18:22

I long to be a woman who follows hard after Jesus. And I'm not talking about a plastic-Christian life, full of religious checklists and pretense. That would be hypocritical at best and deadening at worst.

I want a rich and deep level of intimacy with God that rule-following will never produce. Rules and regulations—lists of dos and don'ts to help sinful people maintain fellowship with a holy God—were an everyday reality for God's people in the Old Testament.

But in the New Testament, Jesus turned everything upside down with His message of grace that declared that following rules wouldn't get us into heaven. He wants us to lay down our checklists and agendas—to lay down everything—and follow Him.

This was a complete shift in thinking. One that left people like the man in Luke 18:22 perplexed. This man, known only as the rich young ruler, approached Jesus and asked Him how he could have eternal life. The man boasted to Jesus about how well he had followed the laws all his life. But Jesus' response shocked him, because Jesus challenged him to sell everything, give it all to the poor, and then follow Him.

It would be so easy to think that Jesus was focused only on the man's material possessions, but He was asking for something far deeper—something the rich young ruler ultimately wasn't willing to give. It's a core requirement for following Jesus. What Jesus wanted most was the man's surrender.

Surrender is not a perfectly lived life like the man in the story boasted about. Surrender is a life fully submitted to God. It tells God that whatever matters most to Him is also what matters most to you. And just like He asked the rich young ruler to surrender it all, that's what Jesus is asking of you and me too. Jesus wants us to completely surrender our lives to Him.

Sweet friend, let's not be like the rich young ruler. Let's not miss out on all God has for us. Let's stop aiming for a perfectly lived life and start living a completely surrendered one.

Please forgive me for all the times when I have settled for lesser things. I want to live surrendered to You, to want You most, and to follow You.

Bring to mind things, people, possessions, or positions that I've held on to too tightly. Help me loosen my grip.

I choose to surrender pursuits that have replaced pursuing You. I want to live in complete abandonment to You. I want to follow hard after You.

IN JESUS' NAME,
AMEN.

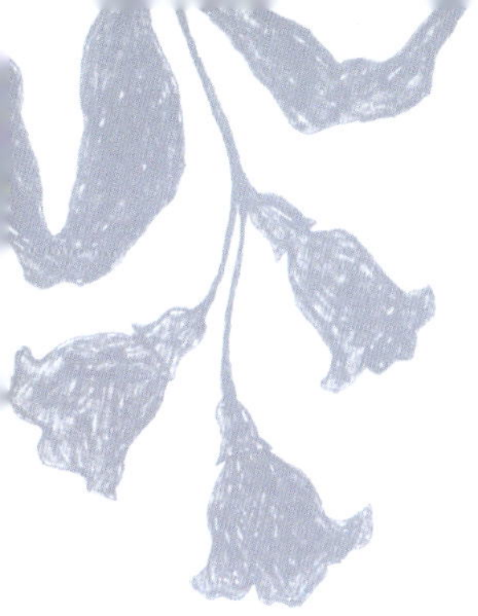

PRAYER IN ACTION

Surrender isn't giving up; it's looking up and letting go with complete trust. As you go about your day, periodically open your hands, palms up, and say, "I release it, Lord; I surrender."

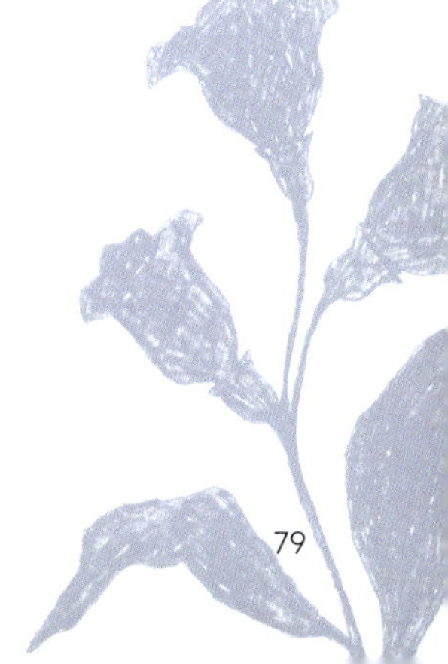

20

UNRUSH ME

A voice from heaven said,

"This is my Son, whom I love; with him I am well pleased."

MATTHEW 3:17

I felt the stress of so many activities and responsibilities pulling at me. Exhaustion dug deep at places in my heart, demanding that I slow down. But how? I had set my life to the rhythm of rush. And it was taking a toll. After all, when a woman lives with the stress of an overwhelmed schedule, she'll ache with the sadness of an underwhelmed soul.

I'm starting to realize that my two most powerful words are *yes* and *no*. How I use them determines how I set my schedule. How I set my schedule determines how I live my life. How I live my life determines how I spend my soul. When I think about my decisions in light of this, it gives gravity to choosing more wisely.

If rushing has become your norm, this is not a time to beat yourself up. Instead, it's a time to make wiser decisions.

Note the timing of God's words to Jesus in Matthew 3:17. At that point, Jesus hadn't yet performed miracles, led the masses, or gone to the cross. Yet God was *already* pleased with Him. His Father was establishing Jesus' identity before Jesus ever started His activities.

Jesus says the same thing to us. He's well pleased because of who we are, not because of what we do.

DEAR LORD,

I confess that I've let activities and obligations drive my schedule. I confess that I haven't stopped to ask You to help me make not just good decisions but God-led decisions.

Give me insight into myself and the choices I make about my activities. Show me when the fear of missing out is motivating me to say yes to things I shouldn't.

I confess that I'm afraid of disappointing people and that being busy sometimes makes me feel more valuable. I've become so accustomed to rushing that sitting still sometimes feels uncomfortable.

I invite You to unrush me. I acknowledge that my activities don't define me or earn more of Your love or approval. You love me because You are Love, and I am Yours.

In You I have the freedom to say no to performance-driven activities and yes to Your assignments. When I'm unrushed, I'll be able to hear Your voice guiding me. I want to embrace Your best for me. I know that's the only place to finally find the deep contentment my soul longs for.

IN JESUS' NAME,
AMEN.

PRAYER IN ACTION

Review today's "to-dos," and choose something you can take off the list—even if it's small. Ask the Lord to help you be more intentional about recognizing things that may not be as urgent as they seem.

21

WAITING TO SEE GOD'S GOODNESS

I remain confident of this: I will see the goodness of the Lord *in the land of the living. Wait for the* Lord*; be strong and take heart and wait for the* Lord*.*

PSALM 27:13–14

Sometimes I attach a great deal of my trust in God to my desire for things to turn out the way I think they should. I want the goodness of God to compel Him to fix things, change minds, prevent hurt, and vindicate me on my timeline.

I want the goodness of God to make life good right now, without any waiting. I want the goodness of God to mean that things turn out okay according to my definition of okayness. I know that the goodness of God means God is good even when everything else isn't. But I have a hard time with this. Especially when there's pain while I'm waiting for God's goodness to be revealed.

And here's my real fear: Sometimes the pain of today feels like a declaration of what my whole future will look like.

I need to press in hard to God with these doubts. I know it's not wrong to have these thoughts. But it's dangerous to let them consume me. With each doubt, we have a choice: Press in hard to God, trusting Him with the unknowns, or pull away. Friend, I pray that you choose to trust God with your story today. He is a trustworthy God. He is trustworthy enough for today and for every day to come.

I confess that I often attach my willingness to trust You to how my life is going at the moment. When things are going my way, it's easy to believe You are trustworthy. But when things fall apart, my trust in You wavers as I struggle to understand what You are doing.

In my quiet moments and time in Your Word, I know that You are good even when my life isn't.

Thank You for reminding me that today is not the end of my story. This will not be my forever.

Today I choose to wait on You. I choose to trust You with what I cannot see, what I do not know, and what I do not want. I give You my fear. I surrender the outcomes and plans I have for the way my life should go to You.

IN JESUS' NAME,
AMEN.

PRAYER IN ACTION

When the thoughts of the not-so-good of today start trying to steal the possibilities of what God can do tomorrow, remind yourself that tomorrow is not an extension of today because His mercies are new every morning.

IF ONLY I HAD . . .

Jesus answered, "Everyone who drinks this water will be thirsty again, but whoever drinks the water I give them will never thirst. Indeed, the water I give them will become in them a spring of water welling up to eternal life."

JOHN 4:13–14

There's a simple yet dangerous script many of us play in our minds, one that holds us back from feeling fulfilled in our relationship with God. It's a script tangled in a lie that typically goes something like this: *I could really be happy and fulfilled if only I had . . . a job I loved . . . a skinnier body . . . more money . . . nicer things . . . a baby . . . a boyfriend or husband . . . a bigger social following . . .*

We all have a version of this script—the result of gaps in our lives, places that feel empty, as if we're missing some crucial piece of the puzzle of our lives.

I don't know what your "if only I had" statements are, but I do know that none of them will bring fulfillment. And if we aren't careful, we may find ourselves praying more for our "if only I hads" than we're praying to have more of Jesus.

It's okay to desire these things, but we shouldn't tie our contentment, security, or identity to them. They can bring moments of happiness, but they can never bring lasting fulfillment or worth, and they certainly can't bring purpose.

We were created for God, so when His Word gets inside us, it not only fills us; it also transforms us. It becomes the new way we process life, rearranging our desires, our motives, our thoughts, and our needs. The more of God we have, the less we need from this world.

Take a quick inventory of your "if only I had" list. Release whatever you're clinging to, and ask God to replace it with a deeper desire for relationship with Him.

I have longed for so many things, thinking if only I had them, I'd be happy. I've let them consume my thoughts, steering me away from You and causing me to be envious of other people. I release these thoughts and ask You to sift them.

Replace them with the things You want me to desire. Make me thirsty for You because only You can quench my thirst in a way that satisfies forever. Fill me with Your truth. Help me stop the "if only I had" cycle, and transform my thoughts by the renewing of my mind through You.

IN JESUS' NAME,
AMEN.

PRAYER IN ACTION

On the left side of a piece of paper, write down your "if only I had" statements. Then across from each item, write an item you can be thankful for. For example, if you write "more updated house" on the left, across from it write, "Thank You, Lord, for the home I do have."

23

LET LOVE MARK YOU

The LORD is close to the brokenhearted and saves those who are crushed in spirit.

PSALM 34:18

It's hard to go through life without getting your heart broken, whether by a parent who didn't love you well, the best friend you thought would never betray you, or the partner who was unfaithful.

When I was a little girl, for many years I wished I knew that my dad loved me. But something was broken in our relationship. That brokenness left me feeling desperate for reassurance. It's painful when the ones who are supposed to love us well don't. Maybe that statement rings painfully true for you too.

It can be so tempting to point to hurts from our past and say, "All my issues can be linked back to what other people did to me." Trust me. I know. It's been more than twenty-five years since I've seen my dad (by his choice). That's hard on a girl's heart. Even a grown girl like me.

I don't know what brokenness from your past still causes you pain today. But I do know that God understands. His Word promises that He is close when our hearts feel so crushed they will never heal. His closeness means you don't have to keep carrying that pain or let it define you.

God is the only One who can heal the hurt our hearts feel.

We can choose not to be marked by what happened to us but instead to be marked by our heavenly Father's love for us. His love is perfect. It will never fail. So today, let's make the choice to rest in the assurance that God is close. And that He loves us completely.

Thank You for being a God who fights for me and delights in me. I haven't always felt that from other people. I've been disappointed and hurt by people who should have loved me.

Thank You for the promise that You are close even when I've been rejected and abandoned by others. I'm so grateful that I'm accepted by You.

I know that this world is broken and that broken things happen. Yet I can't help feeling shattered and disillusioned when heartbreak is a part of my story. Help me to release that pain to You and to trust that You use even the hard things to make me more like You.

Thank You for the promise that You delight over me with singing. Give me ears to hear Your song today and to receive the comfort it brings. Thank You for Your perfect, never-failing love.

IN JESUS' NAME,
AMEN.

PRAYER IN ACTION

You may have noticed that throughout this prayer book, I've used different names to address God in prayer. Today's is "Abba, Father," best translated as "Daddy." Choose one of the names of God that maybe you haven't used before, and say this prayer or your own aloud.

24

BLINDSIDED

A gentle answer turns away wrath,
but a harsh word stirs up anger.

PROVERBS 15:1

Have you ever found yourself reeling from the emotional whiplash of someone's unexpected critical words directed right at you? They always seem to show up at exactly the wrong time.

It was one of those voicemails that left me wondering what to do with all I'd just heard. I was blindsided by the unsolicited criticism. One minute I was enjoying my day, and the next I just wanted to find a hole and crawl into it.

Words hurt. And when someone's critical words hurt us, we can be tempted to let our minds fill with all the possible snippy retorts or, even worse, to let our anger feed critical thoughts about the other person. I'm ashamed to admit that the Jesus-girl thoughts aren't always the first thoughts to rise up in me.

But I've discovered that I have a choice. And I have a perspective shift that can help you: Harsh and unnecessary criticism says a lot more about the other person's insecurities than it does about our inadequacies. This isn't a position of pride but rather a posture of humility that allows us to maintain a pure and compassionate heart when unexpected and hurtful words come our way.

Like the verse today tells us, a "gentle answer turns away wrath." And when we choose not to add more harsh words to the mix, we're able to stay calmer. It helps us pause and ask ourselves questions like, *Did this person intend to help me, or was the intent to hurt me?*

If there's some truth to their words, we should consider a course correction. When we choose not to be defensive, it creates space for a more grace-filled response. We can ask questions like, "Would you help me understand why this is bothering you?" or, "Thank you for caring enough about me to bring this to my attention. What are you hoping I do with this information?"

We can't choose what comes at us, but we can choose to give a gentler response that reflects the gentleness and compassion of God.

Criticism cuts my heart so deeply. Hurtful words can even cause me to be critical or harsh in return. I confess that I let harsh words stick, dwelling on them and ruminating on the ways I want to respond.

Heal my heart of any past critical accusations or comments so my hurt doesn't leak out and hurt others.

Help me keep a clean and pure heart. I want my thoughts about myself and others to be marked by You.

Keep me humble enough not to be defensive and to offer an apology when I need to. I want to be quick to listen and slow to anger.

Help me to receive instruction so I can grow and become more like You. I want my thoughts and my words to be a reflection of You.

IN JESUS' NAME,
AMEN.

PRAYER IN ACTION

When someone's words land like a dagger to your heart, remind yourself that "hurt people hurt people," but you don't have to be one of those people.

A PRAYER OF DECLARATION: THE GOD WHO MAKES THE SUN RISE

I'm reminded of the artistry of our Creator when I'm outside in nature. I love noting the changing pinks and purples of a sunrise or sunset over the marsh. I relish the warmth of oranges and yellows as fall arrives, displaying its glory in the trees. And each day begins and ends with God's display of light and dark.

The consistent rhythms found in nature remind me of this as well—God is consistently true to who He is.

As today's scripture and declaration remind us, God is a God of compassion. God never runs out of His love for us. It's simply a part of our faithful God.

I don't know what you're facing today, but God does. Maybe you can look out the window and see the sunrise. Or walk outside and note the flowers beginning to bloom. Let the beauty of His creation remind you He is faithfully compassionate. He loves you now and tomorrow and each new day.

Because of the LORD's great love we are not consumed, for his compassions never fail. They are new every morning; great is your faithfulness.

LAMENTATIONS 3:22-23

LORD, TODAY I RESIST

the pressure to try to figure out that difficult situation I so desperately want fixed. I resist the desire to control and the temptation to panic and feel like it all depends on me. I resist the pull toward focusing on all that the other person is doing wrong. And I resist dwelling on worst-case scenarios.

Tonight I will stand outside during sunset, and as the light drops into the horizon, I will watch what God puts on display to see what He can do with a mix of light and darkness.

And I will remember why I am not afraid that the end of this day means the end of the light forever.

It's because I know how magnificent it will be when He brings the light back tomorrow morning. I know the sun will rise because God faithfully shows us that over and over and over.

The God who makes the sun rise is the same God to whom I can safely release all I am facing.

God, I know You see all of it. I know You know what to do with it. I trust You to guide me.

I will do my part, and I will let You handle the rest.

IN JESUS' NAME, AMEN.

PRAYER IN ACTION

Which part of today's declaration spoke most personally to you? Write that (or the whole declaration) on a piece of paper, and put it in a place you'll see throughout your day. Speak it to yourself or aloud every time you see it or it comes to mind. You can even send it to a friend who could use these truths today.

A LETTER FROM LYSA

DEAR FRIEND,

If we were grabbing coffee today, I hope you would order whatever made your heart happy. Since I don't drink fancy coffee, I might grab tea. Or maybe I'd order a slice of coffee cake with the plainest coffee they have just to balance out the sweetness of said cake. Then, I'd be eager to get on with our conversation.

I'd want us both to share something we're facing in our lives and then do a check-in about how we're trusting God with this situation. I want to have this kind of conversation more often with my friends.

Sometimes I say I trust God. And I know I've prayed, but unless a friend presses me a little more, I might not admit my prayers are more filled with my ideas for solutions and fear than they are with my trust in Him. I trust Him with some things, but I'm a little more hesitant with other things in my life. I find that I hand something to God in a quick prayer, but then hours later, I'm working behind the scenes again trying to steer, direct, and control things only God can control. This only leads to more fear and anxiety, which leads to me overthinking everything.

In 1 Thessalonians 5:17, we're told to pray continually. This is the perfect prompting to help me keep praying when spiraling feelings start creeping into my mind. It's at that exact moment when I need to stop trying to fix things and refocus my heart and mind on letting the Lord do what only He can do. Prayer is our opportunity to keep handing things we are facing over to Him again and again.

I haven't mastered this by any means, so I give you full permission to do this check-in with me. And I'll do the same for you. Let's pray continually. It's our lifeline.

BE WITH HIM

He appointed twelve that they might be with him and that he might send them out to preach and to have authority to drive out demons.

MARK 3:14–15

Isn't it interesting that Jesus had three years to do a worldwide assignment, yet He never rushed past people to get to the next thing? And He was certainly never too busy for time with His Father. Jesus was into the slower rhythms of life like abiding, delighting, and dwelling—all words used to describe our being with Him.

As a matter of fact, when Jesus appointed the disciples, there were two parts to their calling, as we see in Mark 3:14–15. Yes, they were to go out to preach and to drive out demons, but the first part of their calling was to "be with him." He wants our hearts in alignment with Him before our hands set about doing today's assignment for Him.

So each day, He invites us to be with Him and to receive from Him through worship and prayer and His Word. He wants to give us everything we need for the day while whispering, "This isn't a race to the finish line. I just want you to persevere on the path I have marked out especially for you. Fix your eyes not on a worldly prize but on staying in love with Me."

That's an agenda that's always completely satisfying.

LORD JESUS,

I'm choosing to stop in the midst of everything just to be with You. I don't come with an agenda. I simply want You to know that I love You. I need You. And I want to spend time in Your presence. Remind me, Lord, to do this more often.

I don't want the noise of the world to be what fills my heart and mind. I want You to be the loudest voice in my life . . . the voice of love, reassurance, truth, grace, and peace. Let me never forget what a gift it is to spend this sacred time in Your presence.

IN YOUR NAME,
AMEN.

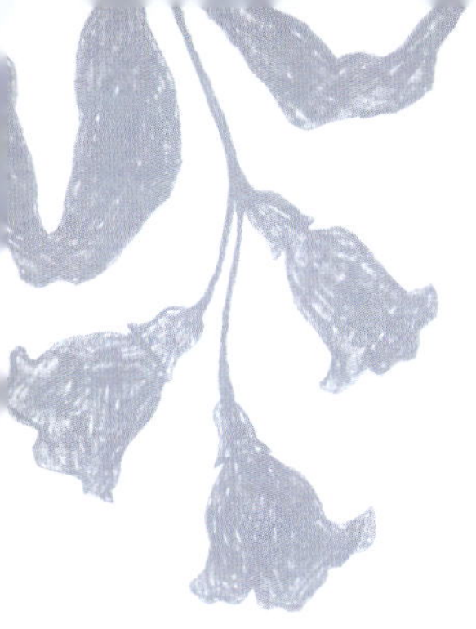

PRAYER IN ACTION

Remember that you can be with Jesus anywhere you are. It doesn't have to be formal or fancy. So as you go about your day today—when you're at a stoplight, in the carpool line, or before you get out of the car while running that errand—pause, take a deep breath, and invite the Lord into that moment with you.

SEND ME!

Then I heard the voice of the Lord saying,
"Whom shall I send? And who will go for us?"
And I said, "Here am I. Send me!"

ISAIAH 6:8

Wherever you are today, know that God has you on assignment. Big or small, it's significant to Him.

The assignment may take you through quiet seasons that cause you to question whether you heard Him correctly. You may feel overlooked and unnoticed or wrestle with doubt. And in the hardest moments, you might even question God: *Why do other people's assignments feel more fast-tracked than mine?* I've been there.

But here's what almost thirty years in ministry has taught me: It's crucial to trust God in the small places. He will meet you there and prepare you there. God's preparing of you in the smaller assignments will be the saving of you in the bigger assignments. And it's not really about the assignment anyway; it's about staying in alignment with His heart.

When Jesus is leading you somewhere that doesn't quite seem to line up with your expectations, remember His words, "Come, follow me" (Matthew 4:19), and say, "Yes, Lord, send me!"

Where is Jesus inviting you to follow Him today? A woman who stays close to Jesus and honors Him with every step—the big ones and small ones—can change the world! I want you to know that you can absolutely be that kind of woman.

Thank You for helping me choose to trust You wherever You lead me. Even when the assignment feels ordinary or insignificant, and I long for something that seems more purposeful, I will say yes to You.

And when Your divine assignment leads me down a scary or challenging path, I won't let fear stop me. I may not always feel brave, but I will find courage in the purpose You have for my life.

I want to do what pleases You. So whatever the assignment, I say, "Yes, Lord, send me." When You guide me, I will go. Help me walk in the specific assignments You have given me—big, small, and every size in between.

IN JESUS' NAME,
AMEN.

PRAYER IN ACTION

Look for ways to say yes to being used by God today, even if it seems insignificant, inconvenient, or scary.

28

HOLD LOOSELY TO OUTCOMES; HOLD TIGHTLY TO JESUS

"Abba, *Father,*" *he said,* "*everything is possible for you. Take this cup from me. Yet not what I will, but what you will.*"

MARK 14:36

Whether you're reeling from a life-altering circumstance, or you're wrestling through something not turning out the way you thought it would, unexpected hard places can leave you hopeless. I know because I've been there too.

The only way I could fall asleep was to lie to myself: *If I can just fall asleep, when I wake up, I'll realize that this is a nightmare that will soon end*. But that wasn't reality. The next morning, I would wake up, and the devastation was there in an even more heartbreaking way.

One thing I want you to know: You are not alone in wanting things to be different and asking God to change your situation. Did you know that even Jesus asked God to change His circumstances and fix what God surely could have fixed in an instant?

Right before He was arrested and eventually crucified, Jesus cried out: "*Abba*, Father . . . everything is possible for you. Take this cup from me" (Mark 14:36).

I have found such comfort in remembering the humanity of Jesus. Yes, His divinity made Him perfect and sinless, but His humanity felt the brutal weight of human hurt. He understands loneliness, devastation, and betrayal by people He should have been able to trust. He knows what it's like to be lied to, misunderstood, falsely accused, and rejected. And because I know He felt what I feel, I know I can trust Him to lead me through whatever I'm facing.

Devastating circumstances have left me weary, confused, and at times hopeless. I never expected to be in this situation. When things in my life feel so uncertain, I am tempted to shrink back in fear or roar forward in control or anger.

Thank You that You understand. When I press into Your love, it leaves me hopeful. Help me to pray like You, "Not what I will, but what You will." You have perspective and insight I don't have, so help me trust You with the unfolding. Especially now, when my life feels so unpredictable, I thank You for the promise that You are the same yesterday, today, and forever.

IN JESUS' NAME,
AMEN.

PRAYER IN ACTION

When you feel hopelessness rise up today, notice your hands, and choose to physically relax your grip. Let God know that you're choosing to hold loosely to your desired outcome and to hold more tightly to Him instead.

29

MY INSECURITIES WON'T WIN TODAY

See what great love the Father has lavished on us, that we should
be called children of God! And that is what we are!

1 JOHN 3:1

It's easy for me to want to avoid the Lord when my shortcomings and insecurities keep surfacing. When I feel I've disappointed Him, it carries over to my prayers. *Here I am again, Jesus, dealing with the same things. I'm disappointed in myself, and I know You must be too. I feel like a failure . . .*

And when we feel like failures, we may be tempted to take it a step further by believing that our perceived failures also diminish our value, which then tempts us to pull back from God even more.

I've discovered that some of the negative thoughts I've let become the soundtrack of my soul actually stem from others who've been critical rather than affirming of me. Maybe you've done that too.

We have to remind ourselves those negative thoughts aren't what Jesus thinks about us.

A few years ago, I volunteered to be the model for a new Proverbs 31 Ministries T-shirt design. It's important to note that I'm usually the last person to volunteer to model anything, but the words on this shirt felt personal: *known and loved*. I knew that taking a picture of me wearing those words would be like a prayer declaring the truth I so desperately needed to believe.

The Enemy wants us to distance ourselves from God, so we must consciously choose to take our thoughts captive and fill our minds with God's thoughts of us. So today, let's invite the One who created us to rewrite the anthem of our identity with His truth.

FATHER GOD,

I love You. Thank You for the truth-filled words of Scripture that remind me that You know and love me, shortcomings and all.

I confess that sometimes I wrestle with negative, critical, or shaming thoughts about myself when I fall short. And I've allowed the voices of others to separate me from You.

I release the lies I've believed that make me feel like less than who You say I am. And right now, I consciously tuck Your whisper of *known and loved* into the deepest part of my heart. I'm so thankful I'm Yours and that Your compassions are new every morning.

IN JESUS' NAME,
AMEN.

PRAYER IN ACTION

Write on a piece of paper, "God sees me and knows me." Tuck it into your pocket or phone case as a reminder that you are fully known and loved by God.

30

UNASHAMED

Then I acknowledged my sin to you and did
not cover up my iniquity. I said, "I will confess my transgressions
to the L*ORD." And you forgave the guilt of my sin.*

PSALM 32:5

Do you ever feel like the hardest person to forgive is actually yourself?

I understand this. Deeply. When I was in my early twenties, I made a decision that I wish with everything in me I could go back and change. I had an abortion. Knowing that nothing could be done to reverse that decision filled me with the deepest kind of despair.

Afterward, every time I heard others talking harshly about abortion, I was filled with shame. It felt like a life sentence I would never be healed from. I would often think, *I can't forgive myself.* What I meant was, *I don't think forgiveness is possible for a person like me. And I don't think I'll ever be free from the shame of what I've done.*

Maybe that's where you are too, with the burden of shame keeping you from coming close to Jesus.

What I eventually learned set me free from trying so hard to forgive myself. The concept of forgiving ourselves is not in the Bible. Forgiveness starts with God. So when we are struggling with forgiveness for ourselves, what's really happening is a struggle to receive and believe in the full forgiveness of God.

Jesus gave His very life to provide forgiveness for our sins, which isn't just part of the Christian faith—it's the very cornerstone of it. Forgiveness for our sins isn't merely a hope we have; it is the greatest reality for all who choose to receive salvation through accepting Jesus as the Lord of their lives.

The weight of shame is by far the heaviest I've ever known, and it's a burden God doesn't want any of us to carry. I'm so thankful that by believing that His death and resurrection take away my sin, with a repentant heart and a prayer of confession, I can be free from this weight of shame, and so can you.

Thank You for paying for my sin and shame on the cross. I confess, repent, and ask You for forgiveness. I want this to be a marked moment when I know that I know that You have forgiven me completely, forever.

I know there will be times when the Enemy tries to condemn me, and I may feel ashamed and guilty again. But I know now that I am shielded by the truth of Your sacrifice and love. I'm thankful today for a fresh revelation of Your grace and mercy.

You promise that when we believe in You, You can use all things for good. If I can ever bring about good by sharing my story, and if I can ever share with someone else that their shame doesn't make them unloved by You, give me the courage to do that.

When we bring sin into Your light, the darkness of the Enemy flees, and shame has no more power over us. Thank You that I now walk in freedom.

IN JESUS' NAME,
AMEN.

PRAYER IN ACTION

If you aren't sure whether you've had a marked moment of asking for God's forgiveness for your sins, or specifically for something you feel ashamed of, pray that now. You can simply pray, "I am weary of the burden of shame. I confess my sin. Thank You that Your death and resurrection fully paid the price of my sin. I know now that I walk in forgiveness and the freedom of Your love. Amen."

WHERE DO I PARK MY THOUGHTS ON A NO-GOOD DAY?

Finally, brothers and sisters, whatever is true, whatever is noble, whatever is right, whatever is pure, whatever is lovely, whatever is admirable—if anything is excellent or praiseworthy—think about such things.

PHILIPPIANS 4:8

It was just too much. Too many people and situations seemed determined to get on my last good nerve. I'll give it to you in two-word snippets and hope you understand. Not that I want you to have a bad day too. But some days you just want someone to say, "I get it," right?

Computer crash. Family drama. Stained pants. Pounds gained. Hormones wacky. Feelings hurt. Tempers short. Dog fleas. Sibling squabbles. Throbbing head. Work deadlines. Urgent errands. No time. Doctor appointment. Waiting room. Waiting room. Waiting room. Messy kitchen. Chores undone. Laundry piles. Paper piles. Dinner flop. Sheer exhaustion.

I could feel my thoughts camping out on, *No one appreciates me; I have to do everything myself; God doesn't care.* And all I could do was go to bed and hope that tomorrow would be better. Long sigh.

When I was typing the title to this, I accidentally typed "a no-God day" instead of what I meant to type, "a no-good day." But then I thought that this is exactly what that day felt like—a no-God day. Not because of God but because of me and the choices I made. I had parked my thoughts on complaints, self-pity, and a negative attitude.

So the next day, instead of just starting where I ended the day before, I spent time confessing my sin to my gracious God. I asked Him to help me think better thoughts on this day, to think about what is true, honorable, right, pure, lovely, admirable, excellent, and worthy of praise.

Grace doesn't give us a free pass to act however we want with no regard for His commands. Rather, His grace gives us consolation on those "too much" days, with a challenge to learn from the situation and to grow each day in becoming more like Jesus and walking closely with Him, no matter what our days are like.

GRACIOUS GOD,

I'm sorry for letting ugly thoughts and a negative attitude take over. Thank You for Your mercy and grace, especially when I know I've messed up. Remind me that You do not want to shame, guilt, or condemn me but to forgive me.

I want to be more like You every day. Help me to turn my thoughts to You more quickly. The minute I feel my thoughts turning to entitlement, self-pity, or feeling unappreciated, help me stop those thoughts immediately with words of what I am thankful for and what I can praise You for.

IN JESUS' NAME,
AMEN.

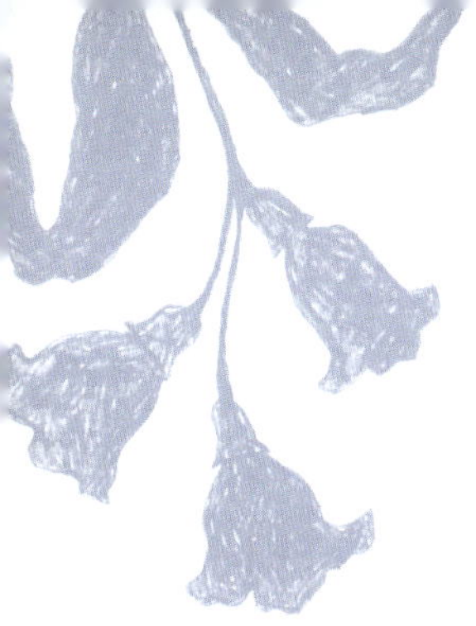

PRAYER IN ACTION

One of the quickest ways to transform your thoughts is to play worship music and sing from your heart. Do that as much as you can today.

32

WHEN I WISH HEALING WERE EASIER

And the God of all grace, who called you to his eternal glory in Christ, after you have suffered a little while, will himself restore you and make you strong, firm and steadfast.

1 PETER 5:10

I want healing to be as neat and predictable as a checklist. I don't want to be caught off guard by the emotions that can go along with it. Of course, if you've ever had to heal from having your heart broken in excruciating ways, you know that you can't schedule healing. You can't hurry it up. And you can't control how and when it will want to be tended to.

When we're healing, loss envelops us with an aching grief that comes in unpredictable waves. It's hard to know if you're getting better when a string of good days suddenly gives way to an unexpected emotional crash.

When my marriage was in shambles, I remember wondering if my heart would ever feel whole again. I believed that God would make something new and wonderful from the dust of my circumstances, even if that didn't include restoring my marriage. But daily functioning while hurting so much was hard.

Gradually, I began to look at those hard days in a different way. Instead of seeing them as setbacks in my healing journey, they became evidence that I was moving through the hardest parts of healing.

Feeling and acknowledging the pain are crucial steps toward healing. All those emotions that keep bubbling up and unexpectedly spilling out? The new tears over old wounds are proof that we're tending to our emotions and processing the grief. We're wrestling well with the ache in our soul.

And while feelings shouldn't be dictators of how we live, they are great indicators of what still needs to be worked through. We must let the ache of sadness and grief ebb and flow around, in, and through us. We have to grant it access to our hearts.

Then one day, we suddenly realize that the future feels like something we might be looking forward to. And one day, it looks stunningly appealing. Not because circumstances have changed but because we have processed emotions, embraced reality, and released control. One step at a time, we're discovering a more healed version of ourselves.

I don't know what kind of pain or heartbreak you may be walking through right now. But I do want to point you toward this hope: Our God is a God of restoration. All the aching within you is proof that there's a beautiful remaking in process. Don't give up. God loves you. You are not alone. Healing is possible.

PRAYER IN ACTION

You might find that journaling is a helpful and healthy way to process your emotions. Get a pretty notebook and write down your thoughts and prayers.

FATHER GOD,

Some days I wish the healing journey was easier. I don't want this heartbreak, and I feel lost in it. But I know You see every tear and know every ache I feel. Thank You that I can be completely honest with my emotions and pour out my heart to You. Help me to trust You to heal my brokenness.

When the weight of my sadness makes it hard to take a step forward, remind me that You are always with me and that You understand.

As I process my emotions, cry out to You, and take small steps forward in healing, please give me Your comfort and peace. Help me to have hope that You will heal me and that You will use all this for my good and the good of others.

IN JESUS' NAME,
AMEN.

THE LORD'S PRAYER

"In this manner, therefore, pray: 'Our Father in heaven, hallowed be Your name. Your kingdom come. Your will be done on earth as it is in heaven. Give us this day our daily bread. And forgive us our debts, as we forgive our debtors. And do not lead us into temptation, but deliver us from the evil one. For Yours is the kingdom and the power and the glory forever. Amen.'"

MATTHEW 6:9–13 NKJV

Jesus didn't leave us trying to figure out the secret to prayer. No, in His abundant goodness toward us, when He taught the disciples how to pray, He was also giving us an example to follow for our prayers.

If you're like me, the Lord's Prayer may be one of those things you've recited and heard much of your life. And while we can certainly find comfort and peace in simply reciting it aloud, Jesus intended it as a guide—like an outline or pattern for us to follow. In it, He teaches us to pray by:

1. Praising our heavenly Father (v. 9).
2. Asking for His will, not ours, for our lives (v. 10).
3. Requesting our daily needs—not focusing on the outcomes we want but instead on things like strength for today or the next step to take (v. 11).
4. Seeking our own forgiveness and giving forgiveness to those who hurt us (v. 12).
5. Asking for God's guidance and protection (v. 13).

I love knowing that the Lord gives us everything we need, even instructions for how to come to Him in prayer. When we follow the pattern of the Lord's Prayer, we can always trust that we are following the example of Jesus.

"May your name be kept holy. May your Kingdom come soon. May your will be done on earth, as it is in heaven. Give us today the food we need, and forgive us our sins, as we have forgiven those who sin against us. And don't let us yield to temptation, but rescue us from the evil one." (Matthew 6:9–13 NLT)

IN JESUS' NAME,
AMEN.

PRAYER IN ACTION

Write out your own prayer, using the five parts of the Lord's Prayer as your guide.

A PRAYER OF DECLARATION: LORD, THANK YOU THAT I CAN COUNT ON YOU

I've had some tumultuous times in the past years. I'm sure you have too, or maybe you're experiencing that time right now. That's part of life, isn't it?

I've been shaken, rattled, dismayed, and shocked at some of the things that people have said and the way they've acted. I've thought many times, *This is not how I imagined my life would look.*

But remember that prayer at the beginning? The one where I'm intentional about seeing God?

Because of that prayer and the way it changes my perspective, I've also seen God's goodness show up again and again. God's goodness is always there—we just have to look for it.

In today's declaration, I've acknowledged these qualities of God I've seen: love, compassion, peace, help, strength, guidance, and forgiveness. Why don't you add to this list and maybe write in your journal about the ways you've seen God show up? End in thankfulness that while our lives may be tumultuous, our God is sure and true.

So we know and rely on the love God has for us.

1 JOHN 4:16

JESUS, I CAN COUNT ON

Your love. Your love is unfailing, unchanging, and unconditional. It's not based on my failures or successes. I can't lose Your love. It's who You are, the God of love.

Jesus, I can count on Your compassion. Your tenderness soothes my heart. Your grace is a gift. Your mercy helps me know that I don't have to hide anything from You and that You provide the truth that sets me free. You keep track of my sadness and bottle up my tears. You know the person or situation that has broken my heart, and I trust that You will help me heal.

Jesus, I can count on Your peace. When the world around me seems unstable, unpredictable, and confusing, Your peace rises above the turmoil and chaos.

Jesus, I can count on Your help. When my anxious thoughts swirl, You bring stillness to my mind. When responsibilities and demands and others' needs overwhelm me, I can turn to You for calmness.

Jesus, I can count on Your strength. When I feel weak and unsure, You give me strength for the situation I'm facing. You are on my side and protect me from human and spiritual enemies. I can trust that You are my refuge.

Jesus, I can count on Your guidance. You are kind in the ways You shepherd me. You lead me with a heart that always wants the best for me and from me.

Jesus, I can count on Your forgiveness. You died a painful, sacrificial death to take on the forgiveness of my sins. You've removed my transgressions as far as the east is from the west. I don't have to beg for forgiveness or try to earn it. I simply accept it with a repentant and thankful heart.

Jesus, thank You that I can count on You now and always.

IN YOUR NAME, AMEN.

PRAYER IN ACTION

Which part of today's declaration spoke most personally to you? Write that (or the whole declaration) on a piece of paper and put it in a place you'll see throughout your day. Speak it to yourself or aloud every time you see it or it comes to mind. You can even send it to a friend who could use these truths today.

SCRIPTURAL PRAYERS

A LETTER FROM LYSA ON SCRIPTURAL PRAYERS

SWEET FRIEND,

As I've shared my heart and we've prayed together, I hope you've experienced God's presence in a new and personal way. I hope these writings and prayers have given you more confidence in His love for you, more grace that your pursuit of Him can be imperfect but still holy, and more ability to focus your heart and mind on Him throughout each day through these new prayer prompts and practices.

This next section will feel a bit different, and while we can absolutely rest in the assurance that God hears *all* our prayers regardless of the words we choose, I didn't want to miss this opportunity to share one of the most powerful types of prayer I've discovered: scriptural prayer.

I believe that when we pray the Word of God, we're praying the will of God.

But I also know that finding just the right verses for what you're facing can be a daunting task, especially when your heart is in the emotional throes of life. So in this section, I've done that step for you. These final prayers are scriptural prayers, categorized by specific needs. All you have to do is pray them, trusting that you're praying truths that are aligned with God's heart. I've even included the verses for deeper study.

I hope you love these prayers as much as I do and that you feel the power of God through them as you pray.

"My word that comes from my mouth will not return to me empty, but it will accomplish what I please and will prosper in what I send it to do."

ISAIAH 55:11 CSB

35

PRAY LIKE JESUS

JESUS PRAYED OFTEN

Heavenly Father, thank You for the example of Jesus' prayer life. He made a habit of thanking You and seeking You in every situation. Help me to rejoice always, pray continually, and give thanks in all things according to Your Word and Jesus' example. Prompt me to get away and pray often like He did.

All that I have is Yours. Thank You for every good and perfect gift You have given me. Thank You for Your miraculous provision. Thank You for Your body, which was broken for me. Thank You for revealing Yourself through Jesus.

Your Word says the gentle and humble-hearted are blessed and will inherit the earth. Teach me to be gentle and humble in heart like Jesus. I want to be an imitator of God. So, like Jesus, I turn my eyes toward You and thank You for hearing my prayer because I know You always hear me. In Jesus' name, amen.

Rejoice always, pray continually, give thanks in all circumstances;
for this is God's will for you in Christ Jesus.

1 THESSALONIANS 5:16–18

Jesus often withdrew to lonely places and prayed.

LUKE 5:16

Very early in the morning, while it was still dark, Jesus got up, left the house and went off to a solitary place, where he prayed.

MARK 1:35

After he had dismissed them, he went up on a mountainside by himself to pray. Later that night, he was there alone.

MATTHEW 14:23

One of those days Jesus went out to a mountainside to pray, and spent the night praying to God.

LUKE 6:12

"All I have is yours, and all you have is mine. And glory has come to me through them."

JOHN 17:10

Every good and perfect gift is from above, coming down from the Father of lights, who does not change like shifting shadows.

JAMES 1:17 CSB

Then Jesus took the loaves, gave thanks to God, and distributed them to the people. Afterward he did the same with the fish. And they all ate as much as they wanted.

JOHN 6:11 NLT

For I received from the Lord what I also passed on to you: The Lord Jesus, on the night he was betrayed, took bread, and when he had given thanks, he broke it and said, "This is my body, which is for you; do this in remembrance of me." In the same way, after supper he took the cup, saying, "This cup is the new covenant in my blood; do this, whenever you drink it, in remembrance of me." For whenever you eat this bread and drink this cup, you proclaim the Lord's death until he comes.

1 CORINTHIANS 11:23–26

At that time Jesus prayed this prayer: "O Father, Lord of heaven and earth, thank you for hiding these things from those who think themselves wise and clever, and for revealing them to the childlike."

MATTHEW 11:25 NLT

"Blessed [inwardly peaceful, spiritually secure, worthy of respect] are the gentle [the kind-hearted, the sweet-spirited, the self-controlled], for they will inherit the earth."

MATTHEW 5:5 AMP

"Take my yoke upon you and learn from me, for I am gentle and humble in heart, and you will find rest for your souls."

MATTHEW 11:29

Therefore, be imitators of God, as dearly loved children.

EPHESIANS 5:1 CSB

So they took away the stone. And Jesus lifted up his eyes and said, "Father, I thank you that you have heard me. I knew that you always hear me, but I said this on account of the people standing around, that they may believe that you sent me."

JOHN 11:41–42 ESV

PRAY LIKE JESUS

JESUS PRAYED FOR HIS FATHER'S WILL

Father God, I know that I must remain close to You for my life to bear godly fruit. I want to be one with You like Jesus; because when I am joined with You, we become one in spirit. Jesus sought You often and did only what You showed Him. I am Your child. Lead me by Your Spirit.

I know that my life is not my own. I want everything I do to come from You. Your Word says that those who listen to You are blessed and will find favor. Let the light of my life shine before others so that it helps reveal You to everyone You place in my path.

My deepest desire is to glorify You and to complete the work You give me. I want to follow John 14:12 by doing the works Jesus did. In all that I do, I seek to please You, so I proclaim the words of Jesus, saying, "Not my will, but Yours be done" in my life. In Jesus' name, amen.

"Remain in me, and I will remain in you. For a branch cannot produce fruit if it is severed from the vine, and you cannot be fruitful unless you remain in me."

JOHN 15:4 NLT

"I pray that they will all be one, just as you and I are one— as you are in me, Father, and I am in you. And may they be in us so that the world will believe you sent me."

JOHN 17:21 NLT

He who is joined to the Lord becomes one spirit with him.

1 CORINTHIANS 6:17 ESV

Jesus said to them, "Truly, truly, I say to you, the Son can do nothing of his own accord, but only what he sees the Father doing. For whatever the Father does, that the Son does likewise."

JOHN 5:19 ESV

Those who are led by the Spirit of God are the children of God.

ROMANS 8:14

Don't you know that your body is a temple of the Holy Spirit who is in you, whom you have from God? You are not your own.

1 CORINTHIANS 6:19 CSB

Blessed is the one who listens to me, watching daily at my gates, waiting beside my doors. For whoever finds me finds life and obtains favor from the LORD.

PROVERBS 8:34–35 ESV

In the same way, let your light shine before others, that they may see your good deeds and glorify your Father in heaven.

MATTHEW 5:16

"I have revealed your name to the people you gave me from the world. They were yours, you gave them to me, and they have kept your word."

JOHN 17:6 CSB

"I have glorified you on the earth by completing the work you gave me to do."

JOHN 17:4 CSB

"Very truly I tell you, whoever believes in me will do the works I have been doing, and they will do even greater things than these, because I am going to the Father."

JOHN 14:12

"By myself I can do nothing; I judge only as I hear, and my judgment is just, for I seek not to please myself but him who sent me."

JOHN 5:30

"Father, if you are willing, take this cup from me; yet not my will, but yours be done."

LUKE 22:42

37

PRAY LIKE JESUS

JESUS PRAYED FOR OTHERS

Dear God, thank You for loving me first. I want to love and pray for others like Jesus. So today, just as He prayed for Simon Peter, I pray that my faith and the faith of others will not fail and that we will strengthen others as we turn to You.

Protect those I love from the schemes of the Enemy, and make them one with You. Sanctify them by the truth of Your Word so they can carry that truth to future generations. Bring them into complete unity with the Father, Son, and Holy Spirit so that others will see Your great love and know that You sent Jesus to give them eternal life.

Your Word says that Jesus was moved by compassion, so I ask You to give me a compassionate heart, and help me to love others just as Jesus did, knowing that love covers a multitude of sins.

Let my life be characterized by both truth and grace so that I can forgive others even when they have hurt me deeply, just as Jesus did from the cross. And I pray that You will make Yourself known to them so that Your love will be in them. In Jesus' name, amen.

We love because he first loved us.

1 JOHN 4:19

"My command is this: Love each other as I have loved you."

JOHN 15:12

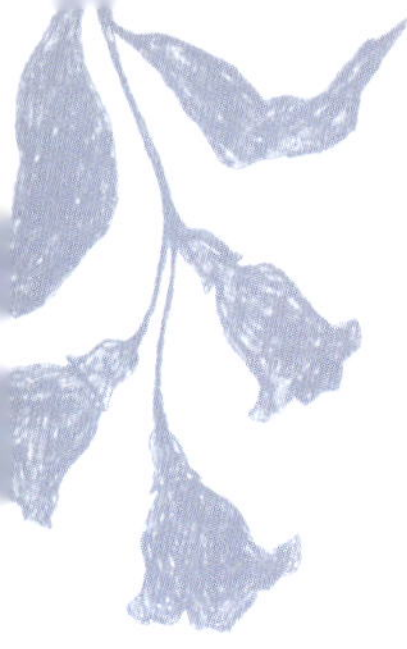

"I have prayed for you, Simon, that your faith may not fail. And when you have turned back, strengthen your brothers."

LUKE 22:32

"My prayer is not that you take them out of the world but that you protect them from the evil one. They are not of the world, even as I am not of it. Sanctify them by the truth; your word is truth. As you sent me into the world, I have sent them into the world. For them I sanctify myself, that they too may be truly sanctified. My prayer is not for them alone. I pray also for those who will believe in me through their message, that all of them may be one, Father, just as you are in me and I am in you. May they also be in us so that the world may believe that you have sent me. I have given them the glory that you gave me, that they may be one as we are one—I in them and you in me—so that they may be brought to complete unity. Then the world will know that you sent me and have loved them even as you have loved me."

JOHN 17:15–23

For God so loved the world that he gave his one and only Son, that whoever believes in him shall not perish but have eternal life.

JOHN 3:16

When he saw the crowds, he had compassion on them, because they were harassed and helpless, like sheep without a shepherd. Then he said to his disciples, "The harvest is plentiful but the workers are few. Ask the Lord of the harvest, therefore, to send out workers into his harvest field."

MATTHEW 9:36–38

When Jesus landed and saw a large crowd, he had compassion on them and healed their sick.

MATTHEW 14:14

When he went ashore, he saw a large crowd and had compassion on them, because they were like sheep without a shepherd. Then he began to teach them many things.

MARK 6:34 CSB

"Don't you believe that I am in the Father and the Father is in me? The words I speak are not my own, but my Father who lives in me does his work through me."

JOHN 14:10 NLT

Above all, love each other deeply, because love covers over a multitude of sins.

1 PETER 4:8

The Word became flesh and made his dwelling among us. We have seen his glory, the glory of the one and only Son, who came from the Father, full of grace and truth.

JOHN 1:14

Jesus said, "Father, forgive them, for they don't know what they are doing." And the soldiers gambled for his clothes by throwing dice.

LUKE 23:34 NLT

"I have made you known to them, and will continue to make you known in order that the love you have for me may be in them and that I myself may be in them."

JOHN 17:26

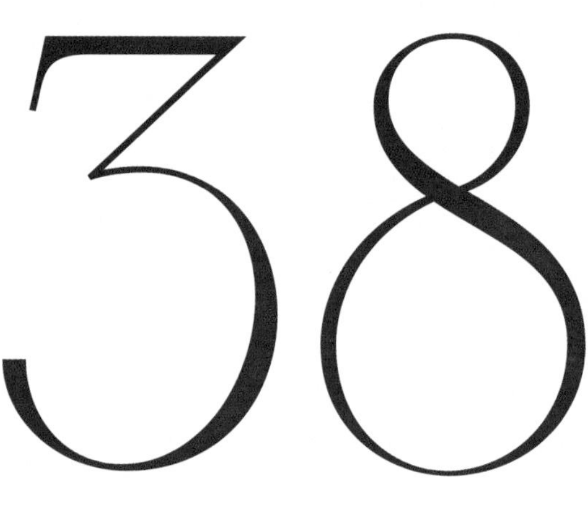

A PRAYER OF PRAISE

Father God, Your Word says that You inhabit the praises of Your people. So even when my soul is downcast, I will put my hope in You and praise You as my Savior and my God. Put a new song of praise and honor in my mouth all day long.

My lips will glorify You. I will lift up my hands and praise You as long as I live because Your love is better than life. The deepest parts of my soul praise Your holy name.

I praise You because You are good, and Your mercy endures forever.

I praise You because I am fearfully and wonderfully made in Your image.

I praise You for revealing Yourself through Jesus.

Yes, Lord, surely I will always have Your praise on my lips. I join with every creature in heaven and on earth and give You all the praise and honor and glory and power forever and ever. In Jesus' name, amen.

Thou art holy, O thou that inhabitest the praises of Israel.

PSALM 22:3 KJV

Why, my soul, are you downcast? Why so disturbed within me? Put your hope in God, for I will yet praise him, my Savior and my God.

PSALM 42:11

He put a new song in my mouth, a hymn of praise to our God. Many will see and fear the LORD and put their trust in him.

PSALM 40:3

My mouth is filled with your praise, declaring your splendor all day long.

PSALM 71:8

Because your love is better than life, my lips will glorify you. I will praise you as long as I live, and in your name I will lift up my hands.

PSALM 63:3–4

Praise the LORD, my soul; all my inmost being, praise his holy name.

PSALM 103:1

Give thanks to the LORD, for he is good. His love endures forever.

PSALM 136:1

I praise you because I am fearfully and wonderfully made;
your works are wonderful, I know that full well.

PSALM 139:14

At that time Jesus said, "I praise you, Father, Lord of heaven and earth, because you have hidden these things from the wise and learned, and revealed them to little children."

MATTHEW 11:25

The Son is the image of the invisible God, the firstborn over all creation. For in him all things were created: things in heaven and on earth, visible and invisible, whether thrones or powers or rulers or authorities; all things have been created through him and for him. He is before all things, and in him all things hold together.

COLOSSIANS 1:15–17

I will bless the LORD at all times;
his praise will always be on my lips.

PSALM 34:1 CSB

Then I heard every creature in heaven and on earth and
under the earth and on the sea, and all that is in them, saying:
"To him who sits on the throne and to the Lamb be praise
and honor and glory and power, for ever and ever!"

REVELATION 5:13

39

A PRAYER FOR PROTECTION FOR YOU AND YOUR FAMILY

Jehovah Nissi (God is my banner), I pray for protection over me and my family. Thank You for being our protector. Psalm 18:2 assures me that I am safe with You because You are a strong fortress, shielding me and defending me.

You keep me from harm by watching over my comings and goings. And You are faithful to deliver me from evil people and guard me from the Enemy.

I can stand in the promise of Isaiah 54:17, which tells me no weapon formed against me will prosper, because, according to Your Word, my battle is not with other people but is against spiritual forces of evil and darkness in heavenly places. I will not fear evil because You are with me. Your rod and Your staff comfort me, and You give me the armor of God to protect me.

I put on the full armor of God now so that I can stand when evil comes. I wrap the belt of truth around me and put on the breastplate of Your righteousness to guard my heart. I declare that my feet are secured with readiness by the sandals of the gospel of peace; and I take up the shield of faith to extinguish the flaming missiles of the Evil One, putting on the helmet of salvation to guard my thoughts and using the sword of the Spirit—which is the Word of God—to pray at all times and keep me alert.

Thank You, Lord, for the victory that I have through Jesus. It's in His name I pray, amen.

> The LORD is my rock, my fortress, and my savior; my God
> is my rock, in whom I find protection. He is my shield,
> the power that saves me, and my place of safety.
>
> PSALM 18:2 NLT

The Lord keeps you from all harm and watches over your life. The Lord keeps watch over you as you come and go, both now and forever.

PSALM 121:7–8 NLT

Pray that we may be delivered from wicked and evil people, for not everyone has faith. But the Lord is faithful, and he will strengthen you and protect you from the evil one.

2 THESSALONIANS 3:2–3

"No weapon forged against you will prevail, and you will refute every tongue that accuses you. This is the heritage of the servants of the Lord, and this is their vindication from me," declares the Lord.

ISAIAH 54:17

Finally, be strong in the Lord and in his mighty power. Put on the full armor of God, so that you can take your stand against the devil's schemes. For our struggle is not against flesh and blood, but against the rulers, against the authorities, against the powers of this dark world and against the spiritual forces of evil in the heavenly realms. Therefore put on the full armor of God, so that when the day of evil comes, you may be able to stand your ground, and after you have done everything, to stand. Stand firm then, with the belt of truth buckled around your waist, with the breastplate of righteousness in place, and with your feet fitted with the readiness that comes from the gospel of peace. In addition to all this, take up the shield of faith, with which you can extinguish all the flaming arrows of the evil one. Take the helmet of salvation and the sword of the Spirit, which is the word of God. And pray in the Spirit on all occasions with all kinds of prayers and requests. With this in mind, be alert and always keep on praying for all the Lord's people.

EPHESIANS 6:10–18

The LORD is my shepherd; I have what I need. He lets me lie down in green pastures; he leads me beside quiet waters. He renews my life; he leads me along the right paths for his name's sake. Even when I go through the darkest valley, I fear no danger, for you are with me; your rod and your staff—they comfort me.

PSALM 23:1-4 CSB

But thanks be to God! He gives us the victory through our Lord Jesus Christ.

1 CORINTHIANS 15:57

40

A PRAYER FOR WHEN YOU NEED HELP WITH A DECISION

Heavenly Father, I don't know what to do, but I look to You, knowing that You declare the beginning from the end of my story. Your desire is for my life to bear good and lasting fruit, so I come to You now, asking for direction.

You see everything. Help me grow in discernment so I can choose what is better. Lead me in the way of truth.

Thank You for the promise that You hear my cries of distress. Your Word tells me that You will answer me, so tune my ears to hear Your wisdom. I desperately want to hear Your sweet words telling me which way to go—lighting my path, showing me where to step.

I want Your best for my life and am willing to obey whatever You show me. In the words of Jesus, I declare, "Not my will, but Yours be done." I submit every part of this decision to You, trusting that Your peace, which surpasses understanding, will guard my mind and heart. You are my Prince of Peace.

I choose not to live in fear of a wrong decision because I know You will go with me *wherever* I go. I commit this decision to You, Lord, and trust that You will establish my plans. In Jesus' name, amen.

"Our God, will you not judge them? For we have no power to face this vast army that is attacking us. We do not know what to do, but our eyes are on you."

2 CHRONICLES 20:12

"Remember the former things, those of long ago; I am God, and there is no other; I am God, and there is none like me. I make known the end from the beginning, from ancient times, what is still to come. I say, "My purpose will stand, and I will do all that I please."

ISAIAH 46:9-10

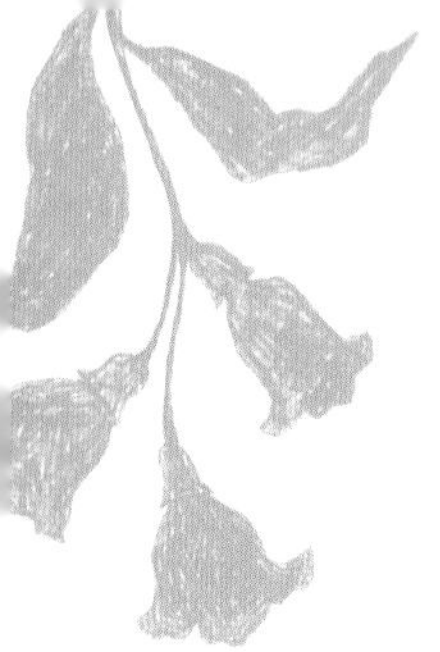

"You did not choose me, but I chose you and appointed you so that you might go and bear fruit—fruit that will last—and so that whatever you ask in my name the Father will give you."

JOHN 15:16

Your ways are in full view of the LORD, and he examines all your paths.

PROVERBS 5:21

I pray this: that your love will keep on growing in knowledge and every kind of discernment, so that you may approve the things that are superior and may be pure and blameless in the day of Christ.

PHILIPPIANS 1:9–10 CSB

Guide me in your truth and teach me, for you are God my Savior, and my hope is in you all day long.

PSALM 25:5

In my distress I called to the LORD; I cried to my God for help. From his temple he heard my voice; my cry came before him, into his ears.

PSALM 18:6

"Call to me and I will answer you and tell you great and unsearchable things you do not know."

JEREMIAH 33:3

Hear my voice when I call, LORD; be merciful to me and answer me.

PSALM 27:7

My child, listen to what I say, and treasure my commands. Tune your ears to wisdom, and concentrate on understanding. Cry out for insight, and ask for understanding. Search for them as you would for silver; seek them like hidden treasures. Then you will understand what it means to fear the LORD, and you will gain knowledge of God. For the LORD grants wisdom! From his mouth come knowledge and understanding.

PROVERBS 2:1–6 NLT

Whether you turn to the right or to the left, your ears will hear a voice behind you, saying, "This is the way; walk in it."

ISAIAH 30:21

Your word is a lamp for my feet, a light on my path.

PSALM 119:105

"If you are willing and obedient, you will eat the good things of the land."

ISAIAH 1:19

"Father, if you are willing, take this cup away from me—nevertheless, not my will, but yours, be done."

LUKE 22:42 CSB

And the peace of God, which transcends all understanding, will guard your hearts and your minds in Christ Jesus.

PHILIPPIANS 4:7

For to us a child is born, to us a son is given, and the government will be on his shoulders. And he will be called Wonderful Counselor, Mighty God, Everlasting Father, Prince of Peace.

ISAIAH 9:6

"Have I not commanded you? Be strong and courageous. Do not be afraid; do not be discouraged, for the Lord your God will be with you wherever you go."

JOSHUA 1:9

Commit to the Lord whatever you do,
and he will establish your plans.

PROVERBS 16:3

A PRAYER BEFORE YOU HAVE A HARD CONVERSATION

Lord, I don't want a bitter root to grow up and cause trouble in this situation. I'm inviting You in, asking You to prepare my heart, mind, and words. Search me first and know my anxious thoughts. Test me and know my concerns. Show me any offensive way or wrong motives within me and wash them away.

Thank You for the comfort of knowing that I don't have to have this conversation alone because You promise not only to go before me but also to go with me.

Help me to speak truth in love, to know when to speak and when to be silent. Keep my heart tender and soft. I want this conversation to honor You, so help the opening of my mouth to produce right things that fit the occasion and offer grace. Let me be quick to listen, slow to speak, and slow to anger.

I will rest in the assurance that nothing is hidden from You because You know everyone's heart. Remind me to keep my focus more on You than on the details of this situation, because when I keep my thoughts on You and trust You, You will keep me in perfect peace. In Jesus' name, amen.

See to it that no one falls short of the grace of God and that no bitter root grows up to cause trouble and defile many.

HEBREWS 12:15

Search me, God, and know my heart; test me and know my anxious thoughts. See if there is any offensive way in me, and lead me in the way everlasting.

PSALM 139:23–24

Wash away all my iniquity and cleanse me from my sin.

PSALM 51:2

"The LORD himself goes before you and will be with you; he will never leave you nor forsake you. Do not be afraid; do not be discouraged."

DEUTERONOMY 31:8

Instead, speaking the truth in love, we will grow to become in every respect the mature body of him who is the head, that is, Christ.

EPHESIANS 4:15

There is a time for everything, and a season for every activity under the heavens . . . a time to tear and a time to mend, a time to be silent and a time to speak.

ECCLESIASTES 3:1, 7

Do not let any unwholesome talk come out of your mouths, but only what is helpful for building others up according to their needs, that it may benefit those who listen.

EPHESIANS 4:29

Nothing in all creation is hidden from God's sight. Everything is uncovered and laid bare before the eyes of him to whom we must give account.

HEBREWS 4:13

Then they prayed, "You, Lord, know everyone's hearts; show which of these two you have chosen."

ACTS 1:24 CSB

You will keep in perfect peace all who trust in you, all whose thoughts are fixed on you!

ISAIAH 26:3 NLT

A PRAYER FOR WHEN YOU FEEL LONELY

Father God, I pray that You would turn and be gracious to me, because I am lonely. Relieve the distress of my heart. I know that You feel my pain and see my trouble. I ask You to satisfy my longing soul and fill me with good things.

Help me see that You are always with me, holding my right hand and guiding me with Your counsel. Your Word says that You are my maker and husband, a father to the fatherless, and a friend that sticks closer than a brother.

Thank You for the promise that even when others forsake me, You take me in and hold me close. You know me because You knit me together in my mother's womb. All my days are written in Your book. Thank You for the assurance that I can never escape Your presence.

James 4:8 promises that when I draw near to You, You come close to me. I know that nothing can separate me from Your love and that You love me with a deep affection, so I cast all my anxiety on You, knowing that You will carefully watch over me.

Thank You for never leaving me, and please help me not be discouraged. Help me to see that You supply all my needs and to know that Your grace is enough for me. I declare that You are my God. You made me. I belong to You, and You belong to me.

God of hope, I trust You. Comfort me and fill me with all joy and peace so that I may overflow with hope by the power of Your Spirit. In Jesus' name, amen.

Turn to me and be gracious to me, for I am lonely and afflicted.
Relieve the troubles of my heart and free me from my anguish.
Look on my affliction and my distress and take away all my sins.

PSALM 25:16–18

For he satisfies the longing soul,
and the hungry soul he fills with good things.

PSALM 107:9 ESV

Yet I am always with you; you hold me by my right hand. You guide me with your counsel, and afterward you will take me into glory. Whom have I in heaven but you? And earth has nothing I desire besides you. My flesh and my heart may fail, but God is the strength of my heart and my portion forever.

PSALM 73:23–26

"For your Maker is your husband—the LORD Almighty is his name—the Holy One of Israel is your Redeemer; he is called the God of all the earth. The LORD will call you back as if you were a wife deserted and distressed in spirit—a wife who married young, only to be rejected," says your God.

ISAIAH 54:5–6

A father to the fatherless, a defender of widows,
is God in his holy dwelling.

PSALM 68:5

One with many friends may be harmed, but there is
a friend who stays closer than a brother.

PROVERBS 18:24 CSB

Even if my father and mother abandon me,
the LORD will hold me close.

PSALM 27:10 NLT

You have searched me, Lord, and you know me. You know when I sit and when I rise; you perceive my thoughts from afar. You discern my going out and my lying down; you are familiar with all my ways. Before a word is on my tongue you, Lord, know it completely. You hem me in behind and before, and you lay your hand upon me. Such knowledge is too wonderful for me, too lofty for me to attain. Where can I go from your Spirit? Where can I flee from your presence? If I go up to the heavens, you are there; if I make my bed in the depths, you are there. If I rise on the wings of the dawn, if I settle on the far side of the sea, even there your hand will guide me, your right hand will hold me fast. If I say, "Surely the darkness will hide me and the light become night around me," even the darkness will not be dark to you; the night will shine like the day, for darkness is as light to you. For you created my inmost being; you knit me together in my mother's womb. I praise you because I am fearfully and wonderfully made; your works are wonderful, I know that full well. My frame was not hidden from you when I was made in the secret place, when I was woven together in the depths of the earth. Your eyes saw my unformed body; all the days ordained for me were written in your book before one of them came to be.

PSALM 139:1-16

Come near to God and he will come near to you. Wash your hands, you sinners, and purify your hearts, you double-minded.

JAMES 4:8

I am convinced that nothing can ever separate us from God's love. Neither death nor life, neither angels nor demons, neither our fears for today nor our worries about tomorrow—not even the powers of hell can separate us from God's love.

ROMANS 8:38 NLT

Casting all your cares [all your anxieties, all your worries, and all your concerns, once and for all] on Him, for He cares about you [with deepest affection, and watches over you very carefully].

1 PETER 5:7 AMP

"Don't be afraid, for I am with you. Don't be discouraged, for I am your God. I will strengthen you and help you. I will hold you up with my victorious right hand."

ISAIAH 41:10 NLT

And my God will supply all your needs according to his riches in glory in Christ Jesus.

PHILIPPIANS 4:19 CSB

But he said to me, "My grace is sufficient for you, for my power is made perfect in weakness." Therefore I will boast all the more gladly about my weaknesses, so that Christ's power may rest on me.

2 CORINTHIANS 12:9

Acknowledge that the LORD is God. He made us, and we are his—his people, the sheep of his pasture.

PSALM 100:3 CSB

You belong to Christ, and Christ belongs to God.

1 CORINTHIANS 3:23 NLT

May the God of hope fill you with all joy and peace as you trust in him, so that you may overflow with hope by the power of the Holy Spirit.

ROMANS 15:13

43

A PRAYER FOR YOUR HUSBAND

Lord, I pray for my husband today. As Romans 12:12–13 instructs us, help him be joyful in hope, patient in affliction, and faithful in prayer. Give him a kind spirit and a tender heart that loves me and our family. I pray that he will always hold our marriage in honor according to Hebrews 13:4 and that You will turn his heart to our children.

Remind him, Lord, to guard his heart above all else so that everything that flows from it is pure, good, and honoring to You and our family. May he also keep his ways pure by living according to Your Word. Help him to always flee from any form of sexual immorality.

I pray that he has wisdom from the Lord that he uses in all his decisions. May he always hold unswervingly to the hope he professes he has in You and never doubt God's faithfulness. Remind him often what Isaiah 41:10 promises: He doesn't need to be afraid or dismayed because You are with him and will help, strengthen, and uphold him.

Let the peace of Christ rule in his heart. May his life be marked by a pursuit of Your heart so that he loves the same things You do. In Jesus' name, amen.

Be joyful in hope, patient in affliction, faithful in prayer. Share with the Lord's people who are in need. Practice hospitality.

ROMANS 12:12-13

Husbands, love your wives, just as Christ loved the church and gave himself up for her.

EPHESIANS 5:25

Give honor to marriage, and remain faithful to one another in marriage. God will surely judge people who are immoral and those who commit adultery.

HEBREWS 13:4 NLT

"He will turn the hearts of fathers to their children and the hearts of children to their fathers. Otherwise, I will come and strike the land with a curse."

MALACHI 4:6 CSB

Above all else, guard your heart, for everything you do flows from it.

PROVERBS 4:23

How can a young man keep his way pure? By
guarding it according to your word.

PSALM 119:9 ESV

Flee from sexual immorality. All other sins a person commits are outside the body, but whoever sins sexually, sins against their own body.

1 CORINTHIANS 6:18

Your word is a lamp for my feet, a light on my path.

PSALM 119:105

If any of you lacks wisdom, you should ask God, who gives generously to all without finding fault, and it will be given to you.

JAMES 1:5

Let us hold unswervingly to the hope we profess,
for he who promised is faithful.

HEBREWS 10:23

Let the peace of Christ rule in your hearts, since as members of one body you were called to peace. And be thankful.

COLOSSIANS 3:15

"But now your kingdom will not endure; the LORD has sought out a man after his own heart and appointed him ruler of his people, because you have not kept the LORD's command."

1 SAMUEL 13:14

A PRAYER FOR YOUR YOUNGER CHILDREN OR GRANDCHILDREN

Abba, Father, thank You for the gift of my children. I know they're a reward from You. Thank You for choosing me to be their earthly mother. I often feel so inadequate, but You, Lord, are more than enough. You are able to give me all that I need at all times.

I pray they would see the great love You have for them and know that they are Your special treasure, created in Your image to do good works.

Help me raise them in the discipline and instruction of Your Word. I pray that they would love others deeply, because love covers a multitude of sins. I want them to know and love You with all their hearts and minds and to call on Jesus as Savior.

Let them hear the sweet lullaby of Your voice delighting over them with singing as You put Your song in their hearts. Build them up with Your wisdom so they will grow and mature in their faith.

I pray that the joy of the Lord will be their strength as You protect them from evil and give them good health. Thank You for being the perfect parent I was never intended to be. In Jesus' name, amen.

Children are a gift from the LORD; they are a reward from him.

PSALM 127:3 NLT

God is able to bless you abundantly, so that in all things at all times, having all that you need, you will abound in every good work.

2 CORINTHIANS 9:8

See what great love the Father has lavished on us, that we should be called children of God! And that is what we are! The reason the world does not know us is that it did not know him.

1 JOHN 3:1

"You are a holy people, who belong to the LORD your God. Of all the people on earth, the LORD your God has chosen you to be his own special treasure."

DEUTERONOMY 7:6 NLT

So God created human beings in his own image. In the image of God he created them; male and female he created them.

GENESIS 1:27 NLT

We are God's handiwork, created in Christ Jesus to do good works, which God prepared in advance for us to do.

EPHESIANS 2:10

Fathers, do not provoke your children to anger by the way you treat them. Rather, bring them up with the discipline and instruction that comes from the Lord.

EPHESIANS 6:4 NLT

Above all, love each other deeply, because love covers over a multitude of sins.

1 PETER 4:8

Jesus replied: "Love the Lord your God with all your heart and with all your soul and with all your mind."

MATTHEW 22:37

They replied, "Believe in the Lord Jesus, and you will be saved—you and your household."

ACTS 16:31

"The Lord your God is among you, a warrior who saves.
He will rejoice over you with gladness. He will be quiet
in his love. He will delight in you with singing."

ZEPHANIAH 3:17 CSB

"The Lord is my strength and my song;
he has given me victory. This is my God, and I will praise
him—my father's God, and I will exalt him!"

EXODUS 15:2 NLT

Jesus grew in wisdom and in stature and
in favor with God and all the people.

LUKE 2:52 NLT

Nehemiah said, "Go and enjoy choice food and sweet drinks, and send some to those who have nothing prepared. This day is holy to our Lord. Do not grieve, for the joy of the Lord is your strength."

NEHEMIAH 8:10

"I am not praying that you take them out of the world
but that you protect them from the evil one."

JOHN 17:15 CSB

Dear friend, I pray that you are prospering in every way and
are in good health, just as your whole life is going well.

3 JOHN 1:2 CSB

A PRAYER FOR YOUR ADULT CHILDREN

Dear Lord, I release my adult children to You, knowing that You are able to guard what You entrusted to me. I pray that they will hold tightly to Your love and the sound teachings of Jesus.

Release them from the generational effects of my and my family's sins so they can rejoice in their inheritance and have everlasting joy.

I pray that You would reveal Yourself to them even when they are not seeking You and help them to grow and mature in their faith.

Strengthen them and protect them from the Evil One. Help them to guard their hearts so that they can flee from all sexual immorality. Lead them to a spouse who loves You and will be a suitable helpmate to them. Surround them with like-minded friends who desire oneness with You so they can encourage one another in their faith.

Proverbs 18:16 says that a person's gifts open doors, so I pray that they discover the gifts You have given them and that the right doors will open for them to use those gifts to serve others and glorify You.

I pray that they will bring their children up in the training and instruction of the Lord and that their children and their children's children will know and follow You.

Help me to know when to speak and when to be silent so that my words will be helpful in building them up according to their needs and Your purposes.

I pray that they will not think they are right in their own eyes but will listen to the advice of many wise counselors so that Your purpose for their life prevails. Thank You that You are their Counselor and will always be their Abba, Father. In Jesus' name, amen.

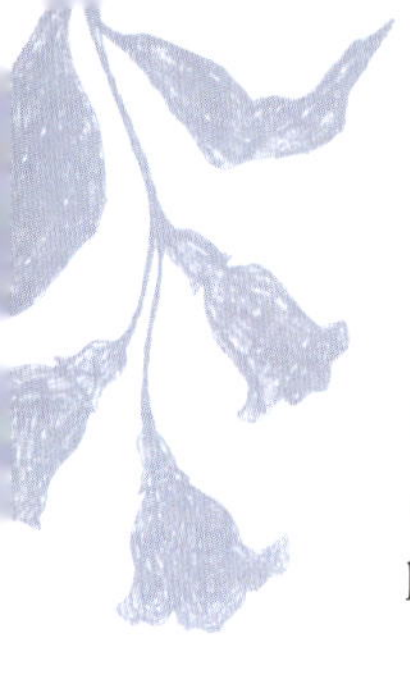

That is why I am suffering as I am. Yet this is no cause for shame, because I know whom I have believed, and am convinced that he is able to guard what I have entrusted to him until that day. What you heard from me, keep as the pattern of sound teaching, with faith and love in Christ Jesus. Guard the good deposit that was entrusted to you—guard it with the help of the Holy Spirit who lives in us.

2 TIMOTHY 1:12–14

"Do not bow in worship to them, and do not serve them; for I, the LORD your God, am a jealous God, bringing the consequences of the fathers' iniquity on the children to the third and fourth generations of those who hate me."

EXODUS 20:5 CSB

In place of your shame, you will have a double portion; in place of disgrace, they will rejoice over their share. So they will possess double in their land, and eternal joy will be theirs.

ISAIAH 61:7 CSB

Later Isaiah spoke boldly for God, saying, "I was found by people who were not looking for me. I showed myself to those who were not asking for me."

ROMANS 10:20 NLT

This will continue until we all come to such unity in our faith and knowledge of God's Son that we will be mature in the Lord, measuring up to the full and complete standard of Christ.

EPHESIANS 4:13 NLT

The Lord is faithful, and he will strengthen you and protect you from the evil one.

2 THESSALONIANS 3:3

Above all else, guard your heart,
for everything you do flows from it.

PROVERBS 4:23

Flee from sexual immorality.
All other sins a person commits are outside the body, but whoever sins sexually, sins against their own body.

1 CORINTHIANS 6:18

Do not be yoked together with unbelievers. For what do righteousness and wickedness have in common? Or what fellowship can light have with darkness?

2 CORINTHIANS 6:14

Then the LORD God said, "It is not good that the man should be alone; I will make him a helper fit for him."

GENESIS 2:18 ESV

Make my joy complete by being like-minded, having the same love, being one in spirit and of one mind.

PHILIPPIANS 2:2

Let us consider how we may spur one another on toward love and good deeds, not giving up meeting together, as some are in the habit of doing, but encouraging one another—and all the more as you see the Day approaching.

HEBREWS 10:24–25

A person's gift opens doors for him and brings him before the great.

PROVERBS 18:16 CSB

We have different gifts, according to the grace given to each of us. If your gift is prophesying, then prophesy in accordance with your faith; if it is serving, then serve; if it is teaching, then teach; if it is to encourage, then give encouragement; if it is giving, then give generously; if it is to lead, do it diligently; if it is to show mercy, do it cheerfully.

ROMANS 12:6–8

Each of you should use whatever gift you have received to serve others, as faithful stewards of God's grace in its various forms.

1 PETER 4:10

Fathers, do not exasperate your children; instead, bring them up in the training and instruction of the Lord.

EPHESIANS 6:4

Our children will also serve him. Future generations will hear about the wonders of the Lord.

PSALM 22:30 NLT

We will not hide these truths from our children; we will tell the next generation about the glorious deeds of the LORD, about his power and his mighty wonders. For he issued his laws to Jacob; he gave his instructions to Israel. He commanded our ancestors to teach them to their children, so the next generation might know them—even the children not yet born—and they in turn will teach their own children.

PSALM 78:4–6 NLT

A time to tear and a time to mend, a time to be silent and a time to speak.

ECCLESIASTES 3:7

Do not let any unwholesome talk come out of your mouths, but only what is helpful for building others up according to their needs, that it may benefit those who listen.

EPHESIANS 4:29

The way of fools seems right to them, but the wise listen to advice.

PROVERBS 12:15

Listen to counsel and receive instruction so that you may be wise later in life.

PROVERBS 19:20 CSB

For to us a child is born, to us a son is given, and the government will be on his shoulders. And he will be called Wonderful Counselor, Mighty God, Everlasting Father, Prince of Peace.

ISAIAH 9:6

"I will be a Father to you, and you will be my sons and daughters, says the Lord Almighty."

2 CORINTHIANS 6:18

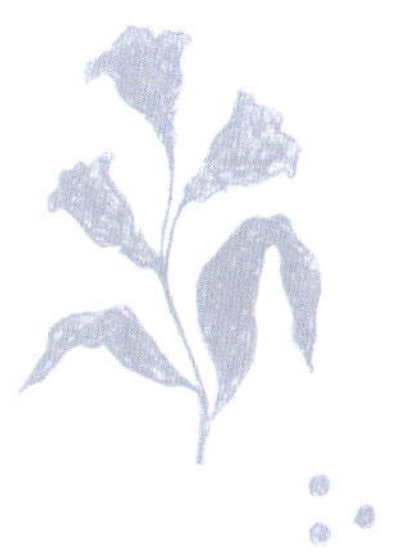

A PRAYER FOR SLEEP AND REST

Dear Lord, I'm weary and tired. Thank You for the promise that I can come to You and You will give me rest. I want to learn from You so I can find rest for my soul.

I cast on You all the worries that keep my mind racing, knowing that You care for me. Thank You that I don't have to stay up late toiling and that You give sleep to those You love. I choose now to be still and know that You are God and to rest in the assurance that You never sleep or slumber. I know that the night watch belongs to You.

Psalm 91:1 promises that when I choose the Most High as my shelter, I can rest in His shadow, so I will not fear the terrors of the night but instead will lie down and sleep in peace, because You alone, Lord, keep me safe.

Thank You for securing me and providing an undisturbed and peaceful resting place so that I can lie down and have sweet sleep with no fear or worry. You are Yahweh-Shalom—the God of peace. In Jesus' name, amen.

"Come to me, all you who are weary and burdened, and I will give you rest. Take my yoke upon you and learn from me, for I am gentle and humble in heart, and you will find rest for your souls. For my yoke is easy and my burden is light."

MATTHEW 11:28-30

Give all your worries and cares to God,
for he cares about you.

1 PETER 5:7 NLT

In vain you rise early and stay up late, toiling for food
to eat—for he grants sleep to those he loves.

PSALM 127:2

He says, "Be still, and know that I am God; I will be exalted among the nations, I will be exalted in the earth."

PSALM 46:10

Indeed, the Protector of Israel does not slumber or sleep.

PSALM 121:4 CSB

On my bed I remember you; I think of you through the watches of the night.

PSALM 63:6

Whoever dwells in the shelter of the Most High will rest in the shadow of the Almighty.

PSALM 91:1

You will not fear the terror of night, nor the arrow that flies by day.

PSALM 91:5

In peace I will lie down and sleep, for you alone, LORD, make me dwell in safety.

PSALM 4:8

My people will live in peaceful dwelling places, in secure homes, in undisturbed places of rest.

ISAIAH 32:18

When you lie down, you will not be afraid; when you lie down, your sleep will be sweet.

PROVERBS 3:24

Gideon built an altar to the LORD there and named it Yahweh-Shalom (which means "the LORD is peace"). The altar remains in Ophrah in the land of the clan of Abiezer to this day.

JUDGES 6:24 NLT

A PRAYER FOR WHEN YOU DON'T KNOW WHAT TO PRAY

Dear Jesus, my heart is desperate, and my mind is so overwhelmed that I can't even put my needs into words. Thank You that I don't have to know what to pray or rely on eloquent and persuasive words for You to hear me. I know that You hear me and that I can rely on the power of Your Spirit at work within me.

Your Word says that when we don't know what to pray, the Holy Spirit prays for us. So I'm asking You, Lord, to intercede for me. And I can rest in the assurance that nothing is hidden from You.

You know every need before I have it. You are my supply, and You're able to do exceedingly and abundantly more than I could ask, think, or imagine. So I declare that I trust in the name of Jesus, knowing that all the promises of God are yes and amen in Him. In Jesus' name, amen.

My message and my preaching were not with wise and persuasive words, but with a demonstration of the Spirit's power.

1 CORINTHIANS 2:4

The LORD hears his people when they call to him for help. He rescues them from all their troubles.

PSALM 34:17 NLT

In the same way, the Spirit helps us in our weakness. We do not know what we ought to pray for, but the Spirit himself intercedes for us through wordless groans.

ROMANS 8:26

There is nothing hidden that will not be disclosed, and nothing concealed that will not be known or brought out into the open.

LUKE 8:17

You know what I am going to say even before I say it, LORD.

PSALM 139:4 NLT

"Do not be like them, for your Father knows
what you need before you ask him."

MATTHEW 6:8

This same God who takes care of me will supply all your needs from his glorious riches, which have been given to us in Christ Jesus.

PHILIPPIANS 4:19 NLT

Now to him who is able to do immeasurably more than all we ask or imagine, according to his power that is at work within us.

EPHESIANS 3:20

Some trust in chariots and some in horses, but we trust in the name of the LORD our God.

PSALM 20:7

For all of God's promises have been fulfilled in Christ with a resounding "Yes!" And through Christ, our "Amen" (which means "Yes") ascends to God for his glory.

2 CORINTHIANS 1:20 NLT

48

A PRAYER FOR WHEN YOU'RE IN A SPIRITUALLY DRY SEASON

Lord, my spirit is like the dry bones whose hope is gone. I come to You knowing that You understand because Your loving-kindness never ceases, and Your compassion never fails. Thank You that I can meet You at the mercy seat and allow Your faithfulness and righteousness to come to my relief.

I repent of allowing other things to take my attention away from You. I turn it back to You now, asking for Your refreshing to wash over me. Your Word says that if anyone thirsts, they should come to You and drink and that, if they believe, living water will come to them.

I believe, Lord, yet forgive my unbelief. I declare now that You, God, are my God. I earnestly seek You. My whole being longs for You in this dry and parched land. You promise to guide me and to satisfy my soul and to make me like a well-watered garden—like a tree planted by a stream, whose roots run deep and do not fear the days of drought.

I choose to fix my eyes firmly on You, Jesus, so that I can be transformed by the renewing of my mind. Although I am faint and weary, I will wait on You and trust that You will renew my strength and raise me up again. In Jesus' name, amen.

Then he said to me: "Son of man, these bones are the people of Israel. They say, 'Our bones are dried up and our hope is gone; we are cut off.'"

EZEKIEL 37:11

Because of the LORD's great love we are not consumed, for his compassions never fail. They are new every morning; great is your faithfulness.

LAMENTATIONS 3:22–23

I will meet with you there above the mercy seat, between the two cherubim that are over the ark of the testimony; I will speak with you from there about all that I command you regarding the Israelites.

EXODUS 25:22 CSB

LORD, hear my prayer, listen to my cry for mercy; in your faithfulness and righteousness come to my relief.

PSALM 143:1

"Repent, then, and turn to God, so that your sins may be wiped out, that times of refreshing may come from the Lord, and that he may send the Messiah, who has been appointed for you—even Jesus."

ACTS 3:19–20

On the last and greatest day of the festival, Jesus stood and said in a loud voice, "Let anyone who is thirsty come to me and drink. Whoever believes in me, as Scripture has said, rivers of living water will flow from within them."

JOHN 7:37–38

"'If you can'?" said Jesus. "Everything is possible for one who believes." Immediately the boy's father exclaimed, "I do believe; help me overcome my unbelief!"

MARK 9:23–24

You, God, are my God, earnestly I seek you; I thirst for you, my whole being longs for you, in a dry and parched land where there is no water.

PSALM 63:1

"The LORD will guide you always; he will satisfy your needs in a sun-scorched land and will strengthen your frame. You will be like a well-watered garden, like a spring whose waters never fail."

ISAIAH 58:11

"They are like trees planted along a riverbank, with roots that reach deep into the water. Such trees are not bothered by the heat or worried by long months of drought. Their leaves stay green, and they never stop producing fruit."

JEREMIAH 17:8 NLT

Fixing our eyes on Jesus, the pioneer and perfecter of faith. For the joy set before him he endured the cross, scorning its shame, and sat down at the right hand of the throne of God.

HEBREWS 12:2

Do not conform to the pattern of this world, but be transformed by the renewing of your mind. Then you will be able to test and approve what God's will is—his good, pleasing and perfect will.

ROMANS 12:2

Youths may become faint and weary, and young men stumble and fall, but those who trust in the LORD will renew their strength; they will soar on wings like eagles; they will run and not become weary, they will walk and not faint.

ISAIAH 40:30–31 CSB

A PRAYER FOR WHEN YOU NEED ENCOURAGEMENT

Jesus, today I'm choosing to rise above the feelings that overwhelm me. I believe that Your blood speaks a better word over me than any failure, fear, or disappointment. I trust that Your Word will prosper in my life and accomplish all You want it to, because You who began the good work in me will continue until it is finished.

I know that You are near, and I earnestly seek You. I have hope because You are my sure and steadfast anchor.

I look to You as the Author and Perfector of my faith. Because of You, I can push back the discouragement of the Enemy, trusting that Your Word is alive and effective in my life. It's sharper than the sharpest two-edged sword.

I will not let trials overcome me. Your grace is sufficient for everything I need. You give me strength and a peace that surpasses understanding. I am chosen and set apart. I find comfort in the knowledge that You will not forget me.

So, I will be strong and take courage in You, knowing that You are making all things new. I choose to trust that Your light and faithful care will lead me. I place my complete confidence in You. In Jesus' name, amen.

And to Jesus, the mediator of a new covenant,
and to the sprinkled blood,
which says better things than the blood of Abel.

HEBREWS 12:24 CSB

"It is the same with my word. I send it out,
and it always produces fruit. It will accomplish all I want
it to, and it will prosper everywhere I send it."

ISAIAH 55:11 NLT

And I am certain that God, who began the good work within you, will continue his work until it is finally finished on the day when Christ Jesus returns.

PHILIPPIANS 1:6 NLT

The LORD is near to all who call on him,
to all who call on him in truth.

PSALM 145:18

This hope is a strong and trustworthy anchor for our souls. It leads us through the curtain into God's inner sanctuary.

HEBREWS 6:19 NLT

Looking away from all that will distract us and] focusing our eyes on Jesus, who is the Author and Perfecter of faith [the first incentive for our belief and the One who brings our faith to maturity], who for the joy [of accomplishing the goal] set before Him endured the cross, disregarding the shame, and sat down at the right hand of the throne of God [revealing His deity, His authority, and the completion of His work.

HEBREWS 12:2 AMP

For the word of God is living and effective and sharper than any double-edged sword, penetrating as far as the separation of soul and spirit, joints and marrow. It is able to judge the thoughts and intentions of the heart.

HEBREWS 4:12 CSB

"I have told you all this so that you may have peace in me. Here on earth you will have many trials and sorrows. But take heart, because I have overcome the world."

JOHN 16:33 NLT

The Lord gives his people strength.
The Lord blesses them with peace.

PSALM 29:11 NLT

And the peace of God, which surpasses all understanding,
will guard your hearts and your minds in Christ Jesus.

PHILIPPIANS 4:7 ESV

But you are a chosen people, a royal priesthood, a holy nation,
God's special possession, that you may declare the praises of him
who called you out of darkness into his wonderful light.

1 PETER 2:9

"Can a mother forget the baby at her breast
and have no compassion on the child she has borne?
Though she may forget, I will not forget you!"

ISAIAH 49:15

Be strong, and let your heart take courage,
all you who wait for the Lord!

PSALM 31:24 ESV

And he who was seated on the throne said, "Behold,
I am making all things new." Also he said, "Write this
down, for these words are trustworthy and true."

REVELATION 21:5 ESV

Send me your light and your faithful care, l
et them lead me; let them bring me to your holy
mountain, to the place where you dwell.

PSALM 43:3

We are confident of all this because of our great trust in God through Christ.

2 CORINTHIANS 3:4 NLT

50

A PRAYER FOR SALVATION (FOR YOURSELF AND OTHERS)

Dear Lord, thank You for salvation and eternal life. Thank You for redeeming me according to the riches of Your grace poured out through Your shed blood on the cross. Please forgive me of all the ways I've fallen short and sinned. I receive the beautiful gift of your mercy and forgiveness. Thank You that even in the midst of my sin, You made a way for me to come to You, and nothing can separate me from Your love.

Your Word says in Romans 10:9 that when "you declare with your mouth, 'Jesus is Lord,' and believe in your heart that God raised him from the dead, you will be saved."

I believe that Jesus is the way, the truth, and the life, and that He is the only way to God.

I believe the promise in 2 Corinthians 5:17 that because I have chosen Christ, I am a new creation—the old me is gone and the new has come. I rejoice because You have clothed me with the garments of salvation and covered me with robes of righteousness.

Your Word says that You want everyone to be saved. So, Lord, I'm asking that all my friends and family will also believe in You and be saved, because Romans 10:20 says that You will be found by those who aren't seeking You and that You will reveal Yourself to those who don't ask.

Reveal Yourself to them, Lord, and rescue them from the domain of darkness, delivering them to the kingdom of Jesus so they, too, will be made new—fully forgiven and redeemed. In Jesus' name, amen.

"There is salvation in no one else! God has given no other name under heaven by which we must be saved."

ACTS 4:12 NLT

For God so loved the world that he gave his one and only Son, that whoever believes in him shall not perish but have eternal life.

JOHN 3:16

In him we have redemption through his blood, the forgiveness of sins, in accordance with the riches of God's grace.

EPHESIANS 1:7

But God demonstrates his own love for us in this: While we were still sinners, Christ died for us.

ROMANS 5:8

I am convinced that neither death nor life, neither angels nor demons, neither the present nor the future, nor any powers, neither height nor depth, nor anything else in all creation, will be able to separate us from the love of God that is in Christ Jesus our Lord.

ROMANS 8:38–39

If you declare with your mouth, "Jesus is Lord," and believe in your heart that God raised him from the dead, you will be saved.

ROMANS 10:9

They replied, "Believe in the Lord Jesus, and you will be saved—you and your household."

ACTS 16:31

Jesus answered, "I am the way and the truth and the life. No one comes to the Father except through me."

JOHN 14:6

Therefore, if anyone is in Christ, the new creation has come: The old has gone, the new is here!

2 CORINTHIANS 5:17

I delight greatly in the LORD; my soul rejoices in my God. For he has clothed me with garments of salvation and arrayed me in a robe of his righteousness, as a bridegroom adorns his head like a priest, and as a bride adorns herself with her jewels.

ISAIAH 61:10

This is good, and pleases God our Savior, who wants all people to be saved and to come to a knowledge of the truth.

1 TIMOTHY 2:3-4

"I was found by those who did not seek me; I revealed myself to those who did not ask for me."

ROMANS 10:20

He has rescued us from the domain of darkness and transferred us into the kingdom of the Son he loves. In him we have redemption, the forgiveness of sins.

COLOSSIANS 1:13-14 CSB

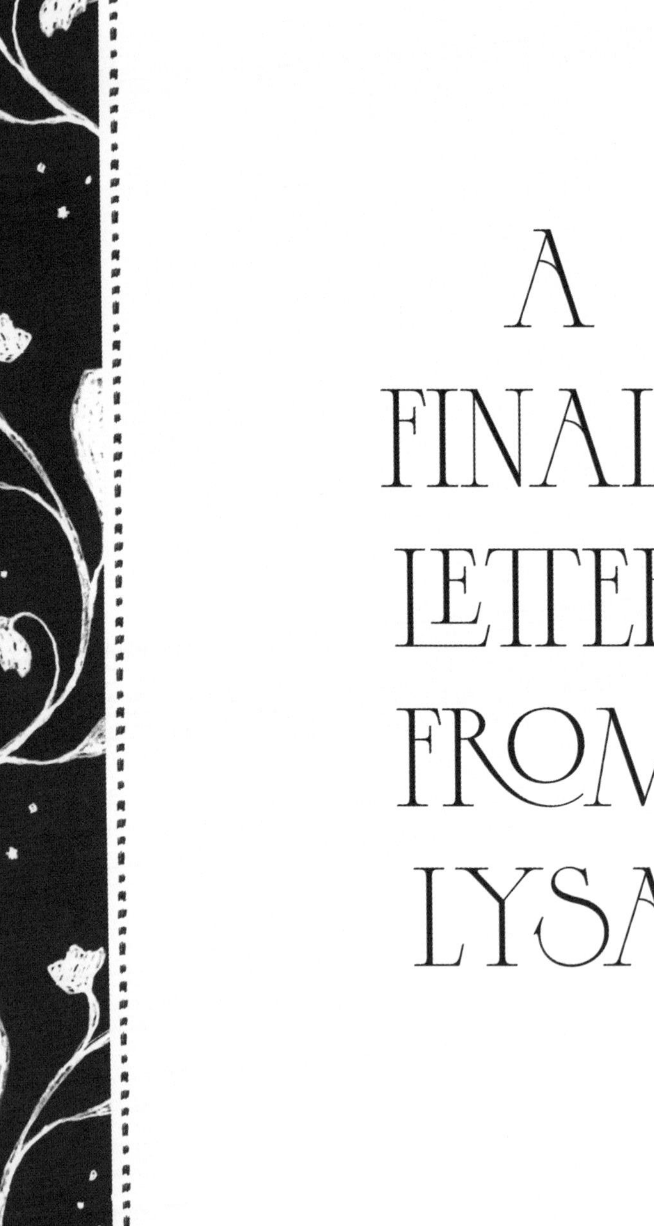

A FINAL LETTER FROM LYSA

SWEET FRIEND,

This book has been a really special project for me. I worked alongside two of my best friends, Mel and Candace, to create what you now hold in your hands. Part of what made it so special was having my friends take my writing and add their wisdom and carefully-prayed-through thoughts.

The other part that has been so special to me is that we didn't just write a book we thought you might need; we journeyed through this message because of our own great need to come close to Jesus.

This has been personally significant for each of us in our own ways. Mel came close to Jesus with her desire for a greater sense of His companionship. Candace brought her desire for clarity, strength, and discernment. And I brought my need for feeling His presence and needing His wisdom.

But mostly, we brought our collective desire to love and be loved by Jesus through the intimate connection of conversations with Him.

Whatever desire you brought to this book, I pray that your heart has been touched by how powerful and how personally tender Jesus is all at the same time.

I hope you are now more assured that He loves you right where you are. He wants to hear our words of praise, thanksgiving, and confession. He wants us to ask for the desires of our hearts. Then He wants us to trust that He knows best and will love us through whatever the outcome is. And most of all, He wants to shape us to be more and more like Him every day.

Jesus is always with you, loving, listening, and leading.

Thank you for letting me walk with you through this. My closing hope for you is simple—that you keep drawing near, keep finding stillness, and keep letting Jesus guide your way . . . one prayer at a time.

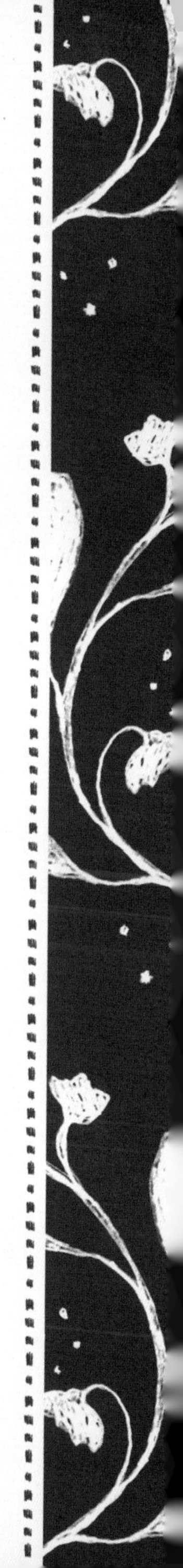

ABOUT THE AUTHOR

LYSA TERKEURST ADAMS is president and chief visionary officer of Proverbs 31 Ministries and the author of eight *New York Times* best-sellers, including *I Want to Trust You, But I Don't*, *Good Boundaries and Goodbyes*, *Forgiving What You Can't Forget*, and *It's Not Supposed to Be This Way*. She enjoys life with her husband, Chaz, and her kids and grandkids. Connect with her at www.LysaTerKeurst.com or on social media @LysaTerKeurst.

Photograph by Kelsie McGarty

ABOUT PROVERBS 31 MINISTRIES

If you were inspired by this book and want to deepen your own personal relationship with Jesus Christ, Proverbs 31 Ministries has just what you are looking for.

Proverbs 31 Ministries exists to be a trusted friend who will take you by the hand and walk by your side, leading you one step closer to the heart of God through:

- The free First 5 Bible study app.
- Free *Encouragement for Today* Devotions.
- *The Proverbs 31 Ministries Podcast.*
- The *Therapy & Theology* podcast.
- COMPEL Pro Writers Training.
- She Speaks Conference.
- Books, Bible studies and other free resources.

Proverbs 31 Ministries desires to help you to know the Truth and live the Truth. Because when you do, it changes everything.

For more information, visit: www.Proverbs31.org.

AN INVITATION FROM LYSA

Photo by Meshali Mitchell

When my family and I were trying to recover from the darkest season of our lives, I prayed one day we would be able to use our experiences to help others find healing. I dreamed of inviting friends like you to my home.

With this vision we built Haven Place, and in recent years hundreds of women have attended our counseling intensives. These are unique retreats with some of the best Christian therapists who specialize in helping women heal from emotional and relational trauma. You'll also have time with Dr. Joel Muddamalle, learning what the Bible says about hard relational topics.

Plus, I'll be there teaching sessions and meeting with you in my living room when we break out into small groups. We limit these intensives to only fifty women with no more than ten to twelve in each small group. These three days will give you the emotional fortitude and biblical confidence to take the next steps toward moving forward in healthy ways.

Healing and hope have become the anthem songs, prayers, and shouts of victory rising from this place that will be a true sanctuary for your heart and soul.

If you'd like more information, visit www.HavenPlace.org.

l Shaddai, God Almighty, I want to tr
fully, wholeheartedly, with everythin
t You know this can wage war wit
desire to be certain, to understan
d to control. It feels like there are
ny unknowns in my life, but thank
that You are constant, the sam
terday, today, and forever. You know
e dreams, desires, and hopes for my fut
en, I want to run ahead of You an
e all these happen. But I don't want t
n on my own understanding; I wa
lean on You. I know the best place
is in Your will. I can count on You t
de me, revealing one step at a time
ether it's a small step or a big one,
and clear. I know that each step o

l Shaddai, God Almighty, I want to t
n fully, wholeheartedly, with everythin
ut You know this can wage war wi
y desire to be certain, to understan
nd to control. It feels like there are
any unknowns in my life, but thank
ou that You are constant, the sa
sterday, today, and forever. You know
ve dreams, desires, and hopes for my fu
ften, I want to run ahead of You an
ke all these happen. But I dont want
an on my own understanding; I w
lean on You. I know the best place
is in Your will. I can count on You
uide me, revealing one step at a tim
hether it's a small step or a big one
clear. I know that each step